An Introduction to Windows Live Essentials

by

N. Kantaris

and

P.R.M. Oliver

Bernard Babani (publishing) Ltd
The Grampians
Shepherds Bush Road
London W6 7NF
England

www.babanibooks.com

Please Note

Although every care has been taken with the production of this book to ensure that any projects, designs, modifications and/or programs, etc., contained herewith, operate in a correct and safe manner and also that any components specified are normally available in Great Britain, the Publishers and Author(s) do not accept responsibility in any way for the failure (including fault in design) of any project, design, modification or program to work correctly or to cause damage to any equipment that it may be connected to or used in conjunction with, or in respect of any other damage or injury that may be so caused, nor do the Publishers accept responsibility in any way for the failure to obtain specified components.

Notice is also given that if equipment that is still under warranty is modified in any way or used or connected with home-built equipment then that warranty may be void.

First Published - November 2009

British Library Cataloguing in Publication Data:

A catalogue record for this book is available from the British Library

ISBN 978 0 85934 710 5

Cover Design by Gregor Arthur

Printed and bound in Great Britain for Bernard Babani (publishing) Ltd

About this Book

In Windows 7 Microsoft has removed several applications that used to come bundled with previous releases of the Windows operating system (OS), and created the 'Windows Live Essentials Suite'. One of the reasons for doing this is to allow Microsoft to update these programs outside the OS. The suite can be downloaded for free and is intended for use with Windows XP, Windows Vista, and Windows 7. The suite is made up of the following main applications:

- **Windows Live Family Safety** – allows parental control of children, who must have a Windows Live ID.
- **Windows Live Messenger** – allows you to get in touch with your contacts by alerting them to your availability online.
- **Windows Live Photo Gallery** – allows you to edit, view, and organise your photos.
- **Windows Live Mail** – allows you to send and receive e-mails and includes Contacts and Calendar.
- **Windows Live Writer** – allows you to maintain a blog or a personal Web site.
- **Windows Live Movie Maker** – allows you to edit home movies and videos and share them with others.
- **Windows Live Toolbar** – is for use with Internet Explorer and provides easy access to several services.
- **Windows Live Outlook Connector** – only appears if you have Microsoft Office installed, making it easier to access Contacts, Calendar and several Windows Live e-mail accounts, and use online collaboration.

An Introduction to Windows Live Essentials is produced in full colour and explains as simply as possible how to use the various applications within the suite, using simple examples when appropriate, and avoiding jargon as much as possible.

About the Authors

Noel Kantaris graduated in Electrical Engineering at Bristol University and after spending three years in the Electronics Industry in London, took up a Tutorship in Physics at the University of Queensland. Research interests in Ionospheric Physics, led to the degrees of M.E. in Electronics and Ph.D. in Physics. On return to the UK, he took up a Post-Doctoral Research Fellowship in Radio Physics at the University of Leicester, and then a lecturing position in Engineering at the Camborne School of Mines, Cornwall, (part of Exeter University), where he was also the CSM Computing Manager. At present he is IT Director of FFC Ltd.

Phil Oliver graduated in Mining Engineering at Camborne School of Mines and has specialised in most aspects of surface mining technology, with a particular emphasis on computer related techniques. He has worked in Guyana, Canada, several Middle Eastern and Central Asian countries, South Africa and the United Kingdom, on such diverse projects as: the planning and management of bauxite, iron, gold and coal mines; rock excavation contracting in the UK; international mining equipment sales and international mine consulting. He later took up a lecturing position at Camborne School of Mines (part of Exeter University) in Surface Mining and Management. He has now retired, to spend more time writing (www.philoliver.com) and developing Web sites.

Trademarks

Contents

Keyboard Shortcuts

General Shortcuts

Ctrl+O	Open	**Ctrl+Shift+J**	Go to Mail
Crtl+S	Save	**Ctrl+Shift+X**	Go to Calendar
Crtl+X	Cut	**Crtl+Shift+C**	Go to Contacts
Crtl+C	Copy	**Crtl+Shift+K**	Go to Feeds
Crtl+V	Paste	**Crtl+Shift+L**	Go to News groups
Crtl+A	Select all	**F1**	Get help
Crtl+P	Print		

Live Photo Gallery

Del	Delete		
Ctrl+M	Rename	**Alt+Enter**	Properties

Live Mail

Ctrl+D	Delete	**Ctrl+Shift+V**	Move to folder
Ctrl+Q	Mark as read	**Ctrl+Shift+A**	Mark all as read
Ctrl+Y	Go to folder	**Alt+Shift+H**	Message in HTML
F9	Block Images	**Ctrl+W**	Manage Newsgroups
Ctrl+R	Reply to sender	**F5**	Sync e-mail accounts
Ctrl+G	Reply to group	**Ctrl+F5**	Sync everything
Ctrl+F	Forward	**Ctrl+Shift+R**	Reply to all

Live Writer

Ctrl+N	New post	**Ctrl+Shift+P**	Publish to blog
Ctrl+G	New page	**Alt+F4**	Close
Ctrl+Z	Undo	**Ctrl+Y**	Redo
Del	Clear	**Ctrl+Shift+C**	Categories
Ctrl+F	Find text	**F2**	Properties
F11	Edit	**Ctrl+F11**	Edit using theme
F9	Task pane	**Shift+F11**	Source
Ctrl+K	Insert hyperlink	**Ctrl+L**	Insert picture
F7	Check spelling		

1

Live Essentials Overview

You can obtain all the **Windows Live Essentials** from several Microsoft Web sites, including:

http://download.live.com/

Read the displayed information (see Fig. 1.1) and when you are ready click the **Download** button.

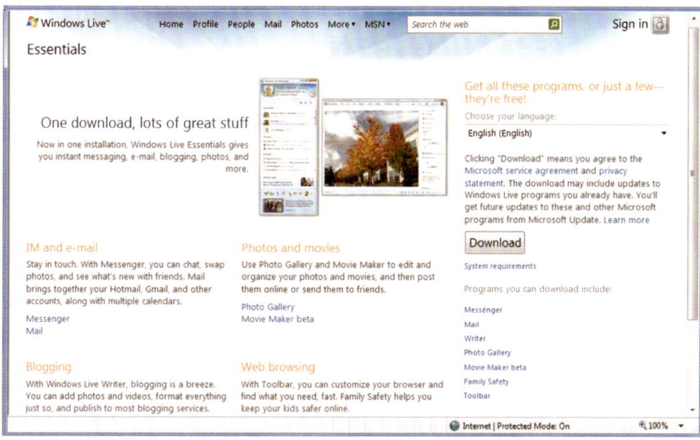

Fig. 1.1 The Windows Essentials Downloading Screen

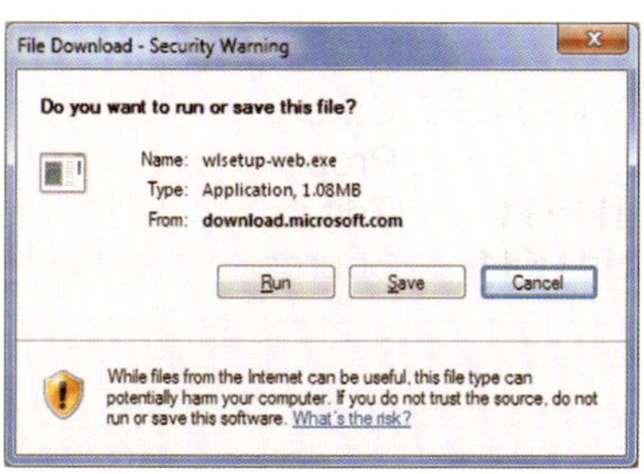

Fig. 1.2 The File Download Box

Next, select **Run** in the displayed dialogue box, shown here in Fig. 1.2. Finally, choose the components that you want downloaded (see Fig. 1.3), and click the **Install** button to download and install them on your PC.

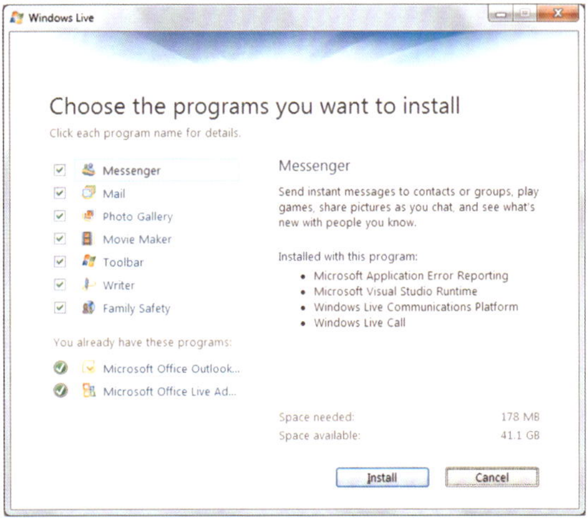

Fig. 1.3 Choosing Windows Essentials Programs

As you highlight each application, as shown Fig. 1.3, an explanation of what the application is about is displayed on the right side of the dialogue box. Clicking the **Install** button starts the download and installation of the selected programs.

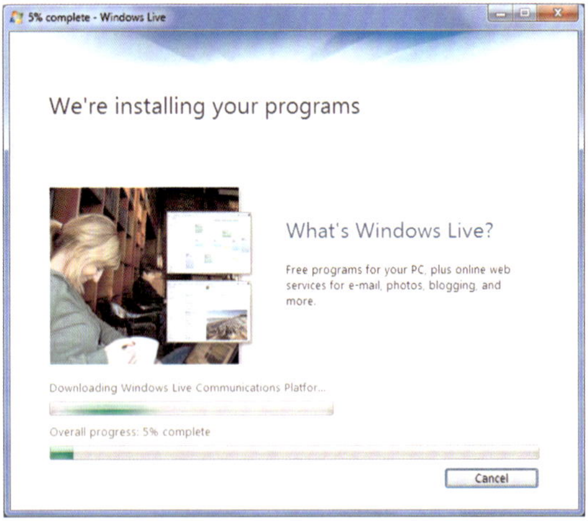

Fig. 1.4 Downloading and Installing Windows Live Essentials

Once all the selected Window Live Essentials have been installed successfully, the following screen is displayed.

Fig. 1.5 Signing Up to Windows Live ID

You will need to set up a Windows Live ID to get the most out of the new Windows Live applications. This is very easy to do; just follow the on-screen instructions. However, if you already use **Hotmail**, **Messenger** or **Xbox Live**, then you already have a Windows Live ID. If not, see the next section.

Note that in the display of Fig. 1.5, you are told that your new applications are to be found in the Windows Live folder in the **Start**, **All Programs** menu, as shown in Fig. 1.6 below.

Fig. 1.6 The Contents of the Windows Live Folder

What these programs can do, is discussed in the last section of this chapter.

Signing Up to a Windows Live ID

If you don't have a Windows Live ID, click the **Sign up** link in Fig. 1.5 to display the following screen.

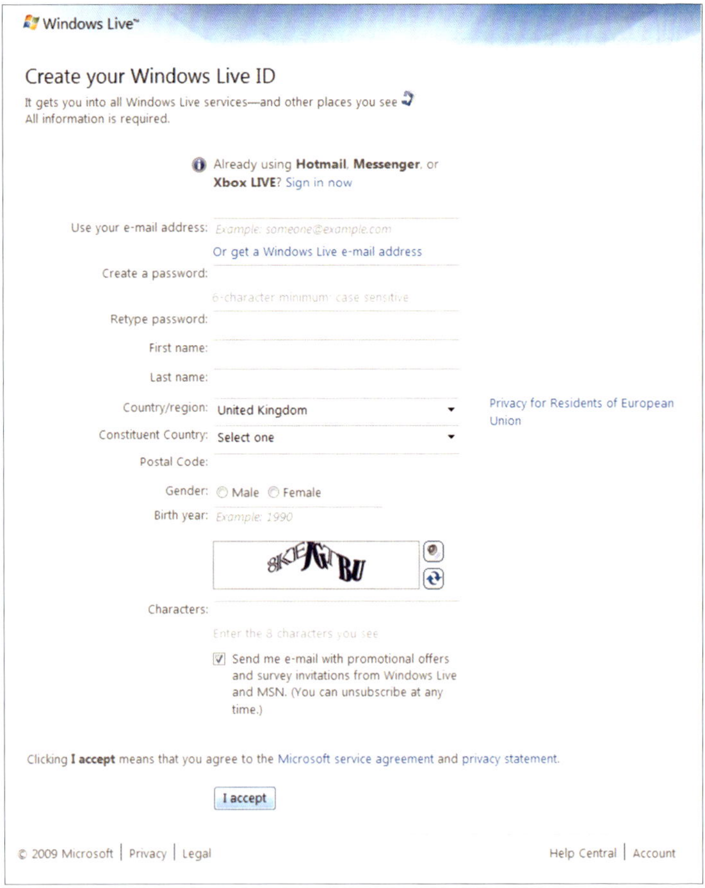

Fig. 1.7 Creating a Windows Live ID

All you have to do is fill in the required information and click the I accept button. Signing up is free. If you find it difficult to make out the 8 characters displayed, click the button to obtain a different combination of characters.

Components of Windows Live Essentials

Windows Live Family Safety

This is parental control by another name. However, every child you wish to protect must have a Windows Live ID registered with Microsoft. You can then control what Websites a child can access.

Windows Live Messenger

This application is the central hub for Windows Live activities online. When a user signs on to Windows Live Messenger, that fact is broadcast throughout the network, alerting your contacts about your availability. From here you can configure information about your Windows Live Profile as well as view information about your contacts.

Windows Live Call

This application integrates into Windows Live Messenger and allows users to make PC-to-PC and PC-to-Phone voice and video calls. Your PC must be equipped with a microphone and speakers and you must have access to a high speed Internet connection for the application to work. It is similar to the popular Skype system, both utilising the Voice over Internet Protocol (VoIP) technology.

Windows Live Photo Gallery

You can view photos by folder, by date taken, by tag (meta data), or by people, using a new People tags feature. You can configure the size of thumbnails, rotate photos in either direction, view them in slide shows, send them by e-mail, print them, and publish them to a variety of services. You can also stitch together two or more photos into a single panoramic view. Photos can be sent to blogs, data CDs, DVDs, and, via Windows Live Movie Maker, into video projects. A support service is Windows Live Sync which allows for PC-to-PC document and Photo synchronisation.

Windows Live Mail

The application includes Contacts and Calendar and is the successor to Outlook Express (XP) and Windows Mail (Vista). Windows Live Mail also replaces Windows Address Book (XP), Windows Contacts (Vista), and Windows Calendar (Vista), and it provides additional functionality in the form of RSS feeds and USENET news-group support.

Windows Live Writer

This application allows you to maintain a blog or a personal Web site. It is by far the easiest blog editor so far, and it works with all the existing blogging services. You can also add video to your posts and it supports photo cropping, tilting, scattering, and borders.

Windows Live Movie Maker

A video editing application that is aimed at the needs of users who want to share their home movies via online services such as YouTube and MSN. The software allows the creation of short home videos from still photos taken by a digital camera or mobile phone, and turns it quickly and easily into a quality product.

Windows Live Toolbar

This is for use with Internet Explorer. There are seven main buttons which give you choices such as What's New, Profile, Mail, Photos, Calendar, MSN, and Share. The What's New option loads a Windows Live Home page, giving you an at-a-glance look at important information such as Mail and Calendar.

Windows Live Outlook Connector

This application only appears if you have Microsoft Office installed. The add-on makes it easier to work with Office Live Workspace – the Microsoft online document collaboration service. The add-on is for Microsoft Outlook 2003 and 2007 and allows a user to access several Windows Live Hotmail-based e-mail accounts, Live Contacts, and Calendar.

The Internet Search Engine Bing

The first thing you'll notice after downloading the Windows Live Essentials suite, signing up to a Windows Live ID, and starting Internet Explorer, is that the MSN portal will open and your favourite Internet search engine has been replaced by **bing**, as shown in Fig. 1. 8 below.

Fig. 1.8 The MSN Portal Page with a **bing** Search Box

This substitution of the Internet Explorer search engine, might be welcomed by some, but not those who prefer their original search engine. However, don't be too hasty in dismissing **bing** before you try it.

As an example we show the results of a search for 'Swine flu masks', first with **bing** (Fig. 1.9), then with Google (Fig. 1.10). We leave it to you to decide which one you prefer.

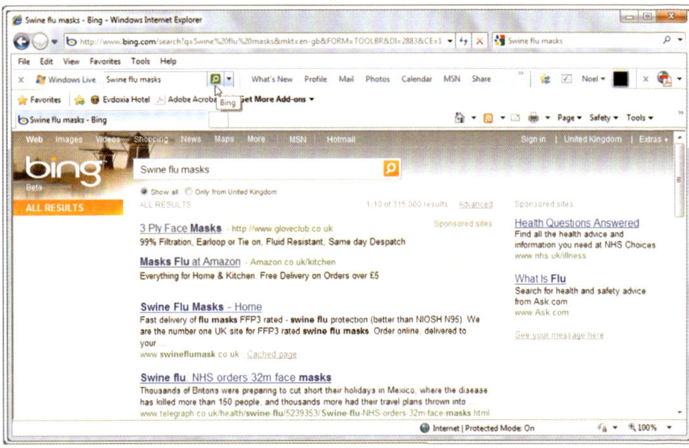

Fig. 1.9 Search Results Using Bing

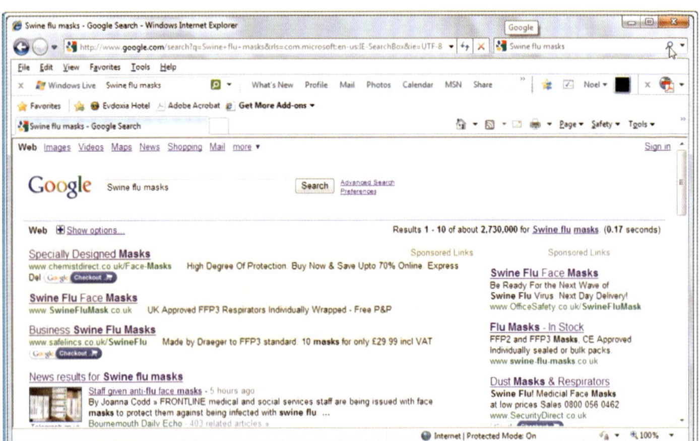

Fig. 1.10 Search Results Using Google

2

Live Safety and Messenger

Family Safety

Fig. 2.1 The Family Safety Task bar Icon

Windows Live takes family safety very seriously. After implementing the program and restarting it, you'll see an icon on the System tray, as shown here in Fig. 2.1.

If a child tries to access an adult site on such a computer (we will show you how to do this shortly), then the Family Safety window will display, as shown in Fig. 2.2.

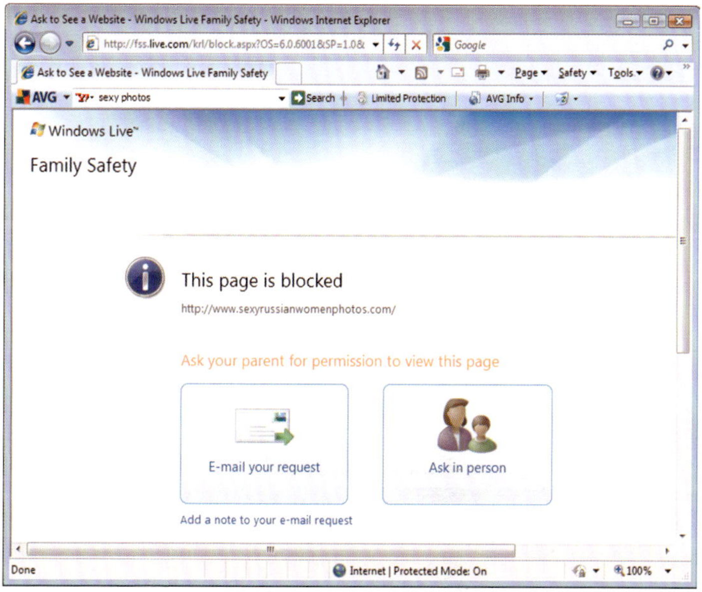

Fig. 2.2 The Family Safety Window

All sites with dubious sexual connotations are blocked automatically, but a child can ask a parent for access to a blocked site by clicking the **Ask in person** button to display a further window in which permission can be given by a parent by signing in and typing their password.

Creating a Family Safety Account

If you have not created a Family Safety Account while installing Windows Live Essentials, you can do so now, but you must have a Windows Live ID. In what follows, we assume that you have already created a **Standard** account for a child (we called it **Johnny)**, using the **start**, **Control Panel**, **Add or remove user accounts** to create it.

Next, click the **Start** button, select **All Programs**, and scroll down and click the Windows Live folder to open it and click the Live Family Safety application to open the window below.

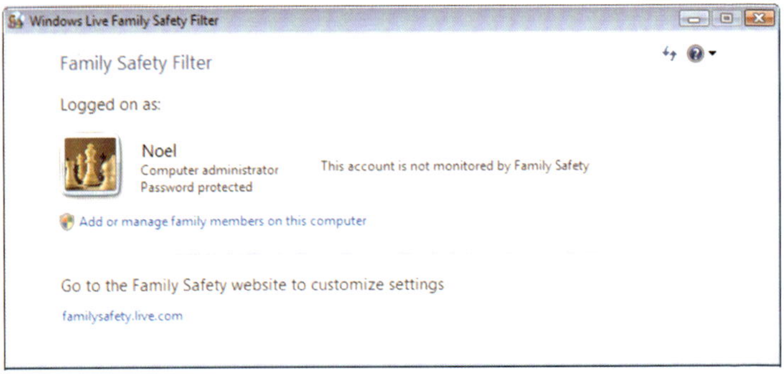

Fig. 2.3 The Family Safety Filter Screen

Now, click the **Add or Manage family members on this computer** link in the above window. You will be asked to sign in with your Windows Live ID, after which the screen shown in Fig. 2.4 on the next page is displayed. In this window we have ticked the account we would like to be monitored by the Live Family Safety application. Clicking **Next** opens a further window as shown in Figure 2.5, also shown on the next page.

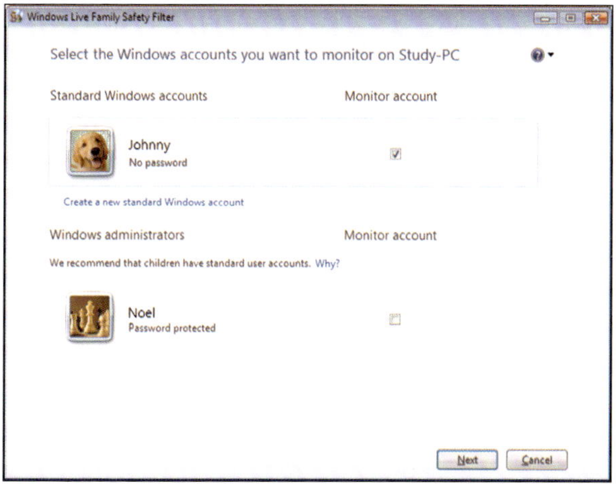

Fig. 2.4 Signing in to Windows Live

Below we have selected from a drop-down list the Family Safety member to be matched with the Windows account.

Fig. 2.5 Matching a Windows Account with a Family Safety Member

Clicking the **Save** button saves the link between Windows account member and Family Safety member and creates a Family Safety Filter. This allows parents to monitor the activities of a child and get reports from the Family Safety Web site.

After restarting your computer a **Family Safety** icon is placed on the System Tray, indicating whether the presently logged user is being monitored or not.

Now clicking the **Family Safety** icon on the System Tray displays the screen in Fig. 2.6 in which you can tell who is currently logged on.

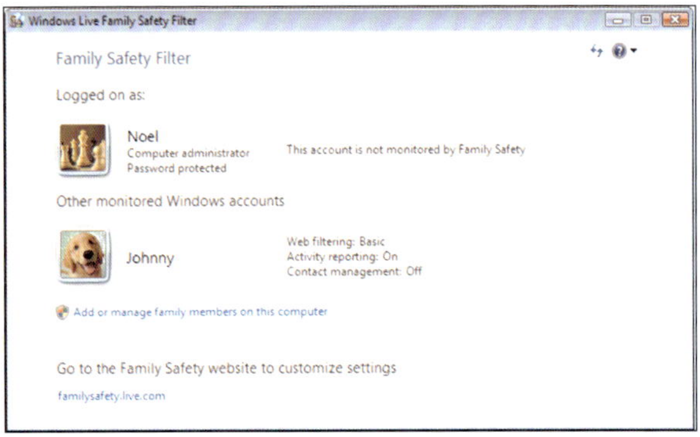

Fig. 2.6 The Family Safety Filter

From here you can go to the Family Safety Web site to customise settings by clicking the **familysafety.live.com** link. This opens the window shown below.

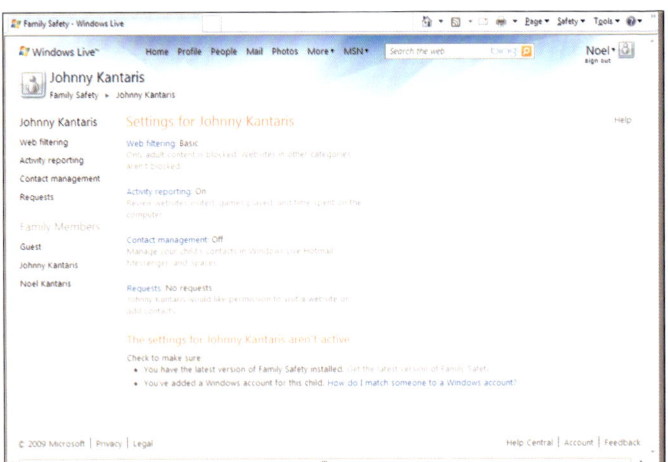

Fig. 2.7 The Family Safety Window for an Individual

From here you can choose what the person stated in the Web filtering screen is allowed to access. The present filtering setting is **Basic** but you can change this to **Strict** or **Custom**. You can also allow or block specific Web sites by providing their Web address.

Clicking the **Contact Management** entry on the left of the screen of the Family Safety window (see Fig. 2.7), allows a parent to control who the child chats and shares e-mail with on Windows Live Hotmail, Messenger, and Spaces.

Removing an Account from Family Safety

To remove an account from Family Safety, click the **Web filtering** entry on the left of the screen of the Family Safety window (Fig. 2.7). This displays additional information for the particular user, as shown in Fig. 2.8 below in which we only show the top part of the displayed window.

Fig. 2.8 The Web Filtering Screen for an Individual

To remove the person in question, select the **Turn off web filtering** option to the far right of the **Web filtering** entry.

If you become the sole user of your computer, you might like to remove Family Safety from your PC altogether. To do so, use the **Start**, **Control Panel**, and click the **Uninstall a program** link shown here.

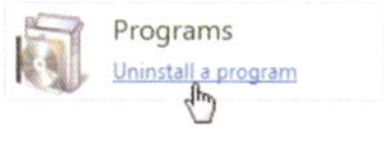

Next, scroll down the list of installed programs and click the Windows Live Essentials entry to select it, then click the **Uninstall/Change** button at the top of your screen.

This displays the Uninstall or repair your Windows Live programs screen, in which you accept the default choice to **Uninstall**. Pressing **Continue**, displays the screen in Fig. 2.9.

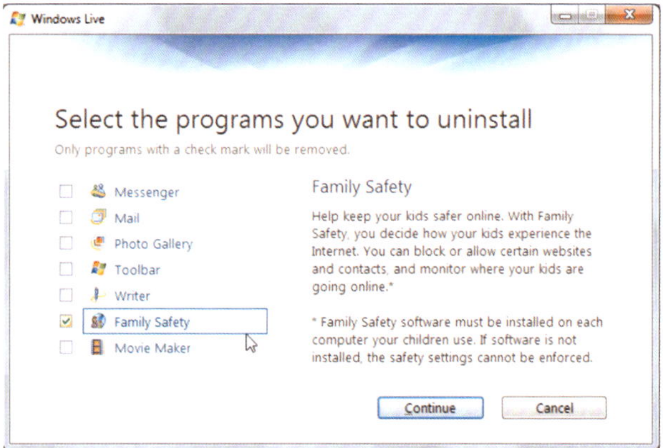

Fig. 2.9 Uninstalling Family Safety from your Computer

Clicking the **Family Safety** box to check it and pressing **Continue**, removes the application from your computer.

Do remember that if in the future you want to control what individual users can access on the Internet, Family Safety must be reloaded on all the computers used in your family!

Live Messenger and MSN Services

Another service that starts when you reboot your PC, is Live Messenger, as shown in Fig. 2.10 on the next page, which lets you talk online, in real time, with friends and family using just a Web browser. You can use it on any shared PC, from school, work, Internet cafe, etc., and can access a variety of services, such as news, weather, money, sport, shopping, games, videos, celebrity gossip, entertainment, etc.

In addition, you can use Live Messenger to share photos with whoever you are having a chat with, right within the same conversation window.

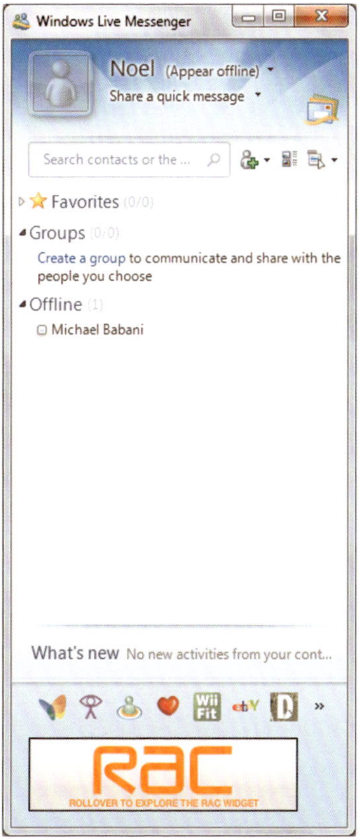

Fig. 2.10 Signing in to Messenger

You have a choice how you sign in, for example, whether you are available or not from the drop-down menu when you click the down-arrow in Fig. 2.10. The choice you have is shown in Fig. 2.11 below.

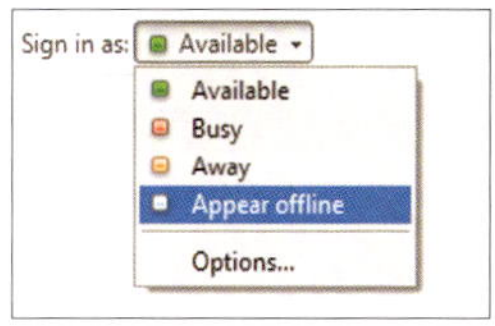

Fig. 2.11 Available Sign in Options

Whether you want to broadcast to everyone to see that you are **Away** is debatable, but if you are busy working you could select the **Busy** option, or if you wanted to see who was online, but not let them know that you were also available online, you could choose the **Appear offline** option.

Finally, Live Messenger provides you with direct access to MSN Hotmail, the free e-mail service for people who do not have a mail account with an Internet Service Provider (ISP). Messages are kept on a server as Web pages and can be accessed from any computer with an Internet connection, anywhere in the world. Of course this service is now provided by Live Mail, which will be discussed in detail later on, but being able to access your Hotmail messages is a bonus.

Having signed in to Live Messenger, click the **Go to Today** icon, at the bottom of the screen to display a similar screen to the one shown in Fig. 2.12 on the next page.

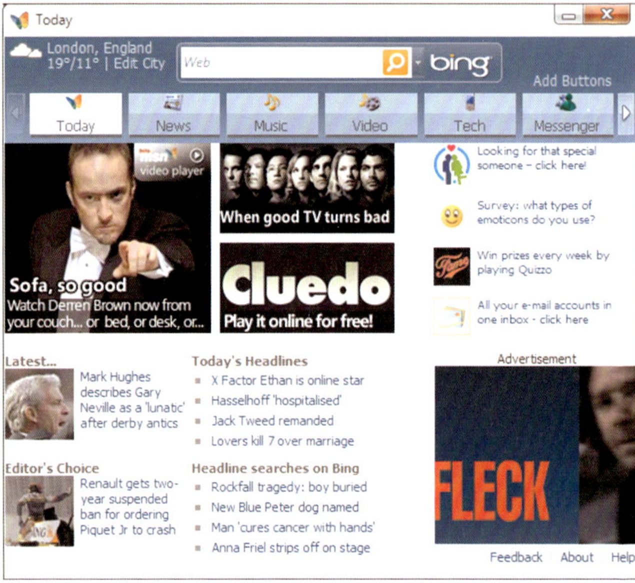

Fig. 2.12 The Windows MSN Screen

What you access here is current news, etc. Obviously the screen shot of Windows MSN will most certainly be different for you, but the services provided should be broadly the same.

Configuring Live Messenger

To make life easier, you can add a **Menu** bar to Live Messenger by clicking the **Show Menu** button and checking the **Show the menu bar** option, as shown in Fig. 2.13 in which we show the action to be taken together with the result of that action.

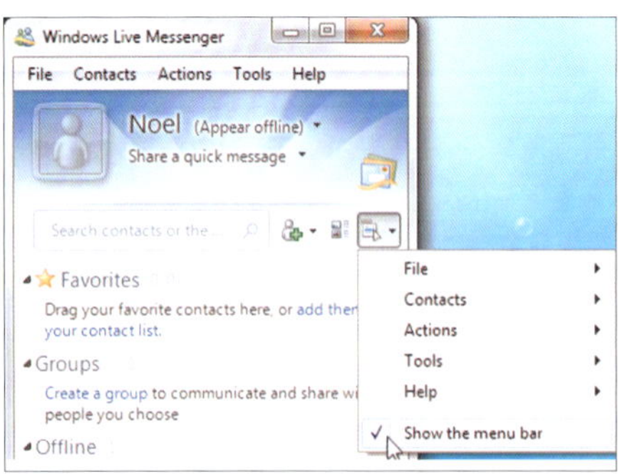

Fig. 2.13 Activating the Menu Bar

Now, with the help of the **Menu** bar, you can make Live Messenger the hub of your activity. Each menu option has a sub-menu associated with it as shown here in Fig. 2.14.

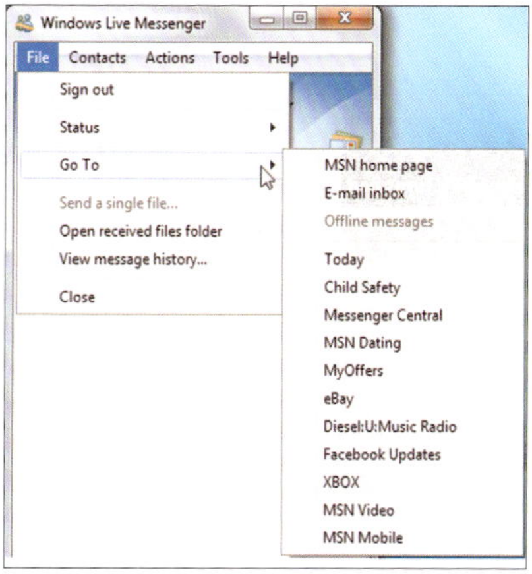

Fig. 2.14 The File Sub-menu

Sub-menu options with a right arrow-head ▸ next to them signify the existence of further options, as also shown open in Fig. 2.14 for the **Go To** sub-menu. From here you can access your e-mail Inbox, eBay, and even get the latest Facebook Updates.

The **Contacts** sub-menu is shown below in Fig. 2.15. From here you can Add, Edit, or Delete a contact, Create a group of contacts, Create, Edit or Delete a Category of contacts, etc.

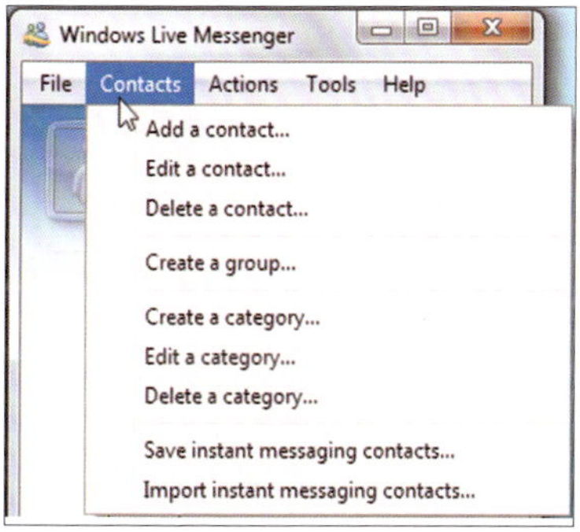

Fig. 2.15 The Contacts Sub-menu

You use Groups in Messenger to enable group chats with up to 20 selected members. On the other hand, if you want to organise people within your contact list, use the categories instead.

To see how you can create a group of contacts, click the **Create a Group** sub-menu option shown in Fig. 2.15. This opens a screen asking you to give the group a name, say, Family Members, School Friends, or something similar – you can create several such groups. Having given a group a name, it is created and the screen in Fig. 2.16 is displayed.

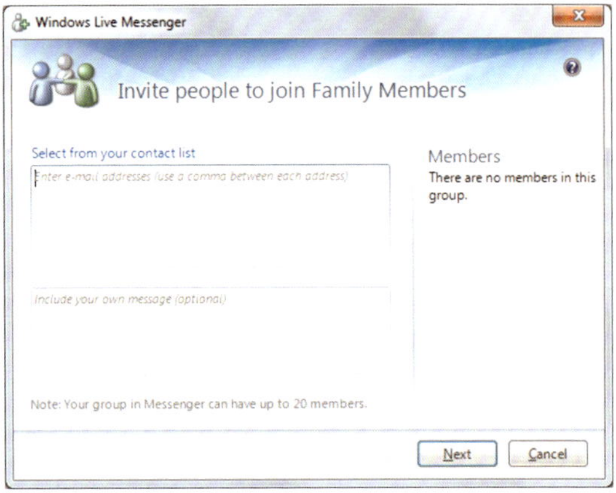

Fig. 2.16 Invitation to Join a Group

Do note that you are asked for two bits of information; the e-mail address of the person you are inviting to join your group, and a comment, such as 'Would you join my group please'. Do supply both of these before clicking **Next**. Obviously to get an instant answer to you invitation, your status should be 'available' (see Fig. 2.11).

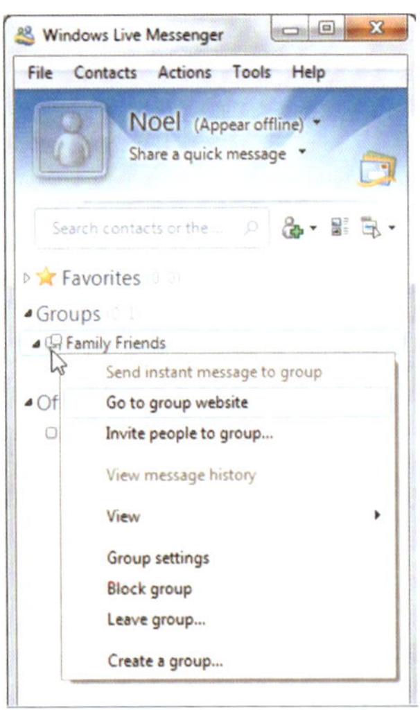

Fig. 2.17 A Named Group

If you made a mistake in choosing the name of the group, then right-click it on Live Messenger where it appears after you have created it, as shown in Fig. 2.17, and select the **Go to group website** option from the drop-down menu also shown open in Fig. 2.17.

This opens the relevant Web page in an Internet Explorer screen, as shown in Fig. 2.18 on the next page, in which we also show the **Options** sub-menu opened by clicking the adjacent down-arrow ▼.

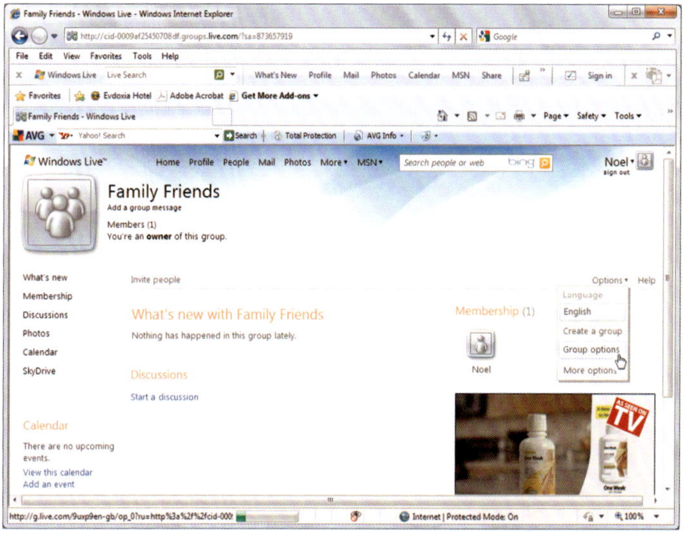

Fig. 2.18 The Group Options Sub-menu

Selecting the **Group Options** sub-menu, displays yet another screen, as shown in Fig. 2.19.

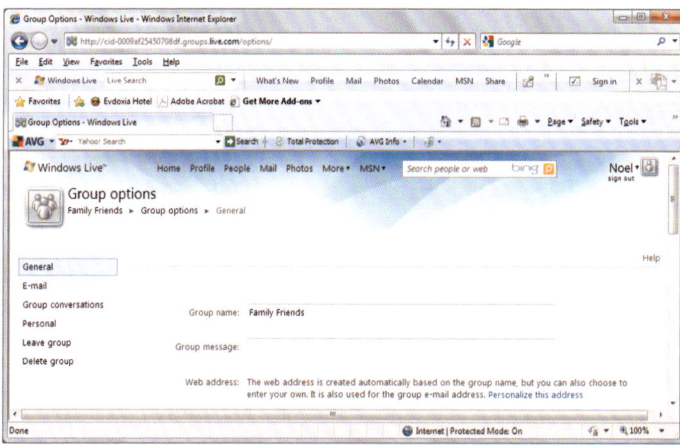

Fig. 2.19 The Group Options Screen

From this screen you can choose to Leave the group, Delete the group, have Group conversations, etc. Try these options.

Below we show the Actions Live Messenger menu options. As you can see, you can use these to send an instant message, send an e-mail, or even send a message to a mobile device. Have a look at what is available.

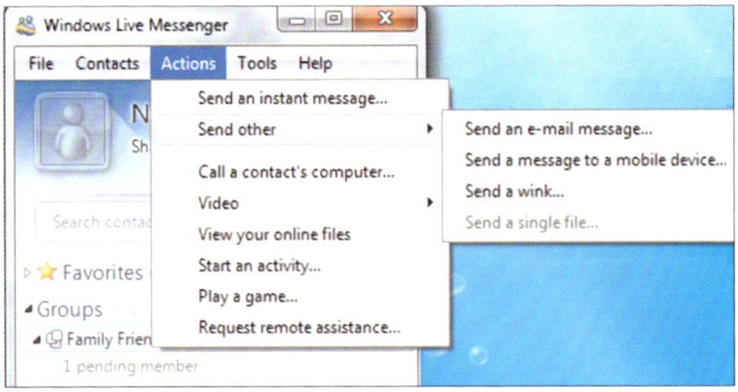

Fig. 2.20 The Actions Sub-menu

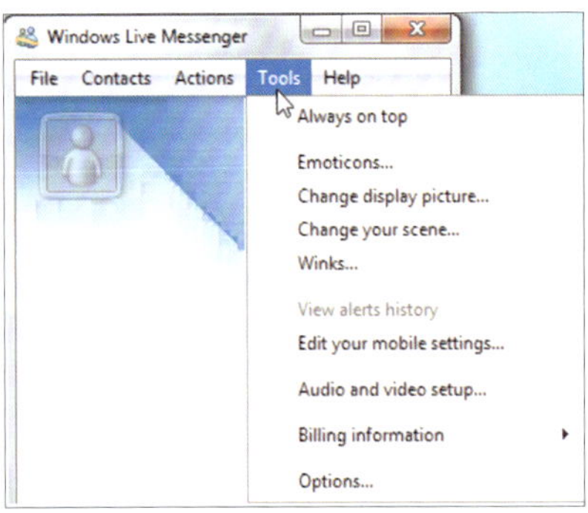

Using the **Tools** sub-menu options, you can add Emoticons and Winks to your messages, and even change your display picture, as shown in Fig. 2.22.

Fig. 2.21 The Tools Sub-menu

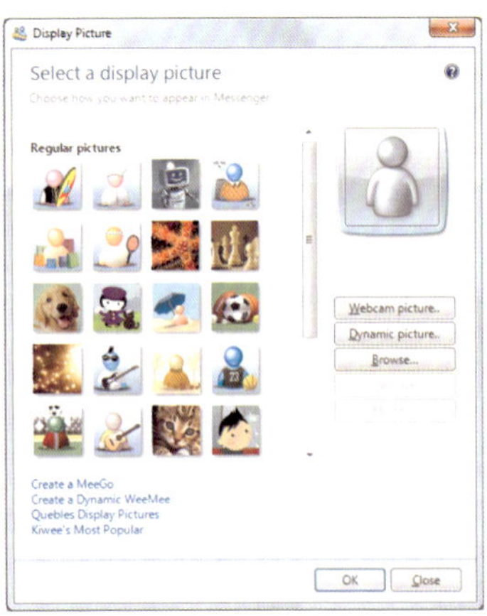

From this Display Picture dialogue box you can either use one of the **Regular pictures**, or click the **Webcam picture** button to activate automatically your PC's Webcam and take a real picture of yourself. Have a look at the **Dynamic pictures** option.

Fig. 2.22 Selecting a Display Picture

Clicking the **Options** sub-menu item under **Actions**, displays the screen shown in Fig. 2.23. From here you can change several options, from Personal to Connection. It might be worth your while spending some time here.

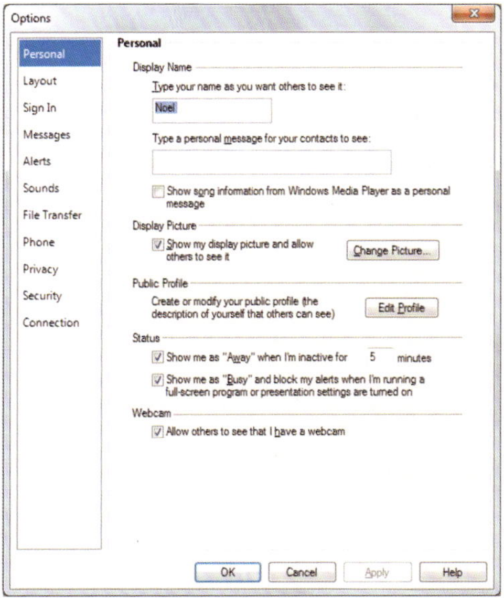

Fig. 2.23 The Tools, Options Sub-menu

Consolidating your Social Network

To bring together all your Web social activities under one umbrella, click the **Add a contact or group** button on Live Messenger and select the **Add people from other services** option from the drop-down menu, as shown here in Fig. 2.24. This opens the screen in Fig. 2.25 on the next page.

Fig. 2.24 Adding Contacts from other Services

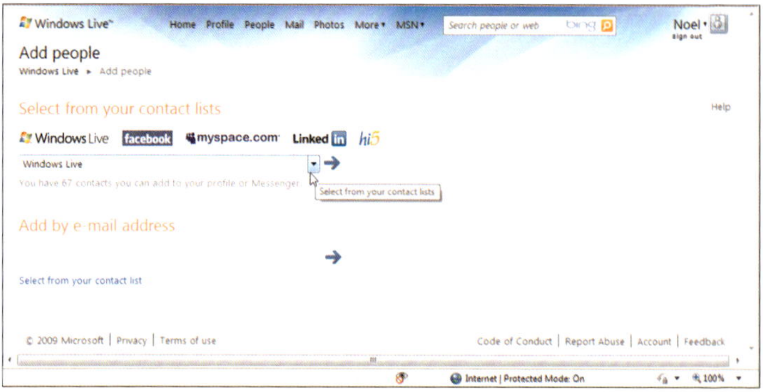

Fig. 2.25 Getting Contacts from Other Web Services

Do spend some time examining the various options and get a friend to co-operate in a Live chat with you, so you can find out how useful it is, before joining larger groups.

The various facilities available to you from Live Messenger, such a Photos, Mail, and others will be discussed in detail in following chapters of the book.

3

Windows Live Photo Gallery

With the **Windows Live Photo Gallery** you can view photos as shown in Fig. 3.1, you can edit them, sort them, and display them in different ways; by date, using star ratings, or using descriptive tags. Once your photos have been fixed and organised, you can save a folder of photos to a blank CD or DVD, or click a button to make a slide show with **Windows Live Movie Maker**.

Fig. 3.1 Windows Live Photo Gallery

To see Windows Live Photo Gallery in operation, click the **Start** button, select **All Programs**, and scroll down and click the Windows Live folder to open it. Now, click the application **Windows Live Photo Gallery** which loads the program and automatically indexes all the photos on your hard drive.

Finally a screen similar to the one shown in Fig. 3.2 below is displayed. As you can see, features offered by Photo Gallery include:

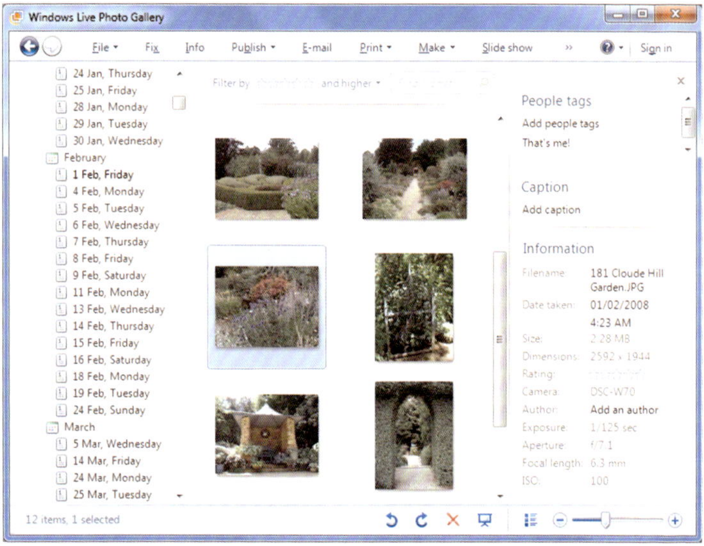

Fig. 3.2 The Windows Live Photo Gallery Window

- Easily finding photos and videos as they are gathered by Photo Gallery in one place and are displayed by date, name, or tag (text attached to a photo or video to describe it). Photos and videos can be sorted by a variety of criteria, such as date taken, People tags, or Descriptive tags, as shown in Fig. 3.3 when the expanded left panel of Fig. 3.2 is shrunk.

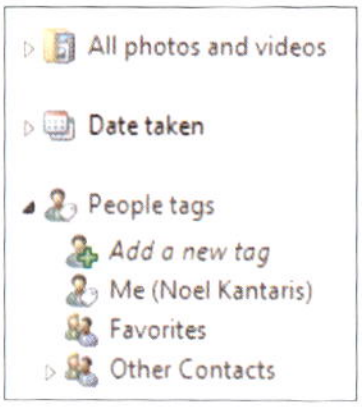

Fig. 3.3 Sort Criteria

To do this, scroll to the very top of the left panel and click the inclined blue arrowhead pointed to in the displayed screen to the right. We find that sorting our photos by date is by far the best and most logical option, but some people might have the time to name each photo or give it a tag or star rating.

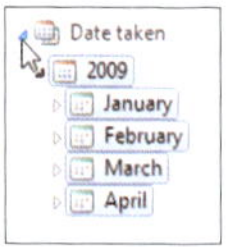

- Import photos and video files from a digital camera or video camera, a scanner, CDs and DVDs, and from the hard disc of your PC.
- Edit and enhance photos by fixing their colour and exposure, cropping, and removing the appearance of red eye caused by the flash reflecting off a person's eyes. You can also use Photo Gallery to combine photos into a panoramic view, and add captions.
- Share your photos and videos by publishing them on Windows Live Spaces, create online slide shows, or e-mail them to friends and family.

The Photo Gallery Window

When Photo Gallery first opens you will see that it lists all of your photos by date and has retained the same file structure as your hard drive, as shown for us in Fig. 3.2.

To understand Photo Gallery it is important to remember that the program scans your computer for photos, and displays them for you. It does not keep, copy, or store, your photos, they are always maintained in their original files on your hard disc. But it does keep and process references to them which it stores in its own database. **If you delete a photo from a folder in Photo Gallery, the photo will be deleted from the folder on your computer.** So beware!

On the left of the Photo Gallery window (Fig. 3.2) is a Folders List pane, with the main working area, or library, to the right displaying thumbnails of the images in the selected folder. To explain what thumbnails can be seen at any given time, use the scroll bar to the immediate right of the Folders List pane and scroll to the very top of the list. What should now appear on your screen is something similar to what is shown for us in Fig. 3.4 on the next page.

In Fig. 3.4 we have also left-clicked the Public Pictures folder which opened up the folder to reveal all the sub-folders contained in that folder, and at the same time selected all the sub-folders as shown in the display on the next page.

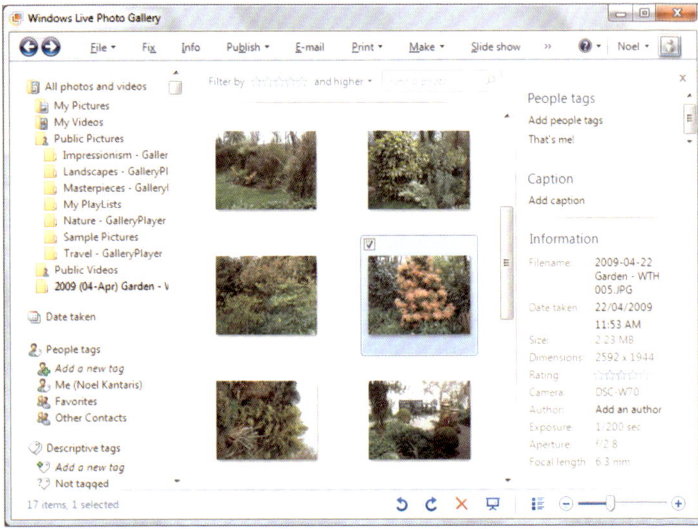

Fig. 3.4 The Public Pictures Photos

Although the thumbnails are grouped by the folders and sub-folders on your hard disc, you can continuously scroll through thumbnails of the selected folder and its sub-folders, using the scroll bar on the right of the thumbnails panel, or by rolling your mouse wheel. So in the working area you can access any photo on your computer without having to physically open its folder.

To move quickly through a large number of photos, locate the folder you want in the Folders List on the left and click it. To scroll through all your photos on your hard disc, click the name of the folder in which you keep them. In our case this is the Photos folder on an external hard disc. We have such a large collection of photos that we prefer to keep them separately from the few held in My Pictures folder. In your case it could be that all your photos are held in the My Pictures folder.

In Fig. 3.5 on the next page, we show what happens when the folder containing all our pictures is clicked. As you can see, all the sub-folders are automatically selected which means that we can scroll through all our pictures.

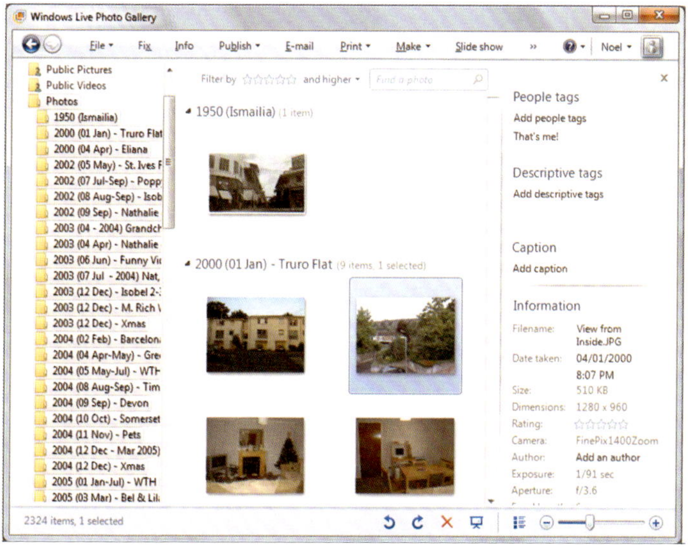

Fig. 3.5 The Folder Containing all our Pictures

Although you can continuously scroll through your folders of thumbnails, you always know where you are in the list as a header is placed above each group of thumbnails as shown above. Note that selecting the folder that contains all your photos, lists all the sub-folders within it in ascending chronological order, as shown in Fig. 3.5, while clicking the **Date taken** option on the Folders List, displays folders and sub-folders in ascending chronological order, as shown in Fig. 3.2.

On the right of the thumbnail area the Information pane is displayed. It lets you know the name of the highlighted picture, the date and time it was taken, the size and dimension of the photo. This pane can be closed by either clicking the close button x or clicking the **Info** menu option. To display this pane again, click the **Info** button once more.

To change the size of the thumbnails, use the slider below the Info pane. Moving the Slider towards the ⊕ sign increases the thumbnail size and display fewer thumbnails, while moving it towards the ⊖ sign, reduces the thumbnail size, allowing more thumbnails to be displayed.

Organising your Photos

How you organise your photographs is obviously a personal choice. Some people just put them all into one folder, such as My Pictures folder and use Photo Gallery to separate them into date order. We prefer to create a new dated folder for every batch of photos we download from our camera, such as those shown in Fig. 3.5, then it is easier to sort the folders in date order.

To permanently delete a photo from your computer using Photo Gallery, just right-click its thumbnail and select **Delete** from the context menu. Clicking **Yes** in the Confirmation box will send it to the Windows Recycle Bin.

Tags and Stars

Rather than physically move all your photos, you can give them 'tags' or 'stars', and search for photos with these attributes when you want them. You could tag all the photos of friends and family with their names for instance. In Photo Gallery you can add multi-word tags to your photos and they are stored in the actual photo files themselves.

To add a tag, select your photo and click the **Add people tags** button to open the **People tags** window shown in Fig. 3.6 below. Next type a name in the text box provided and click the **Add new person** button pointed to in the composite display.

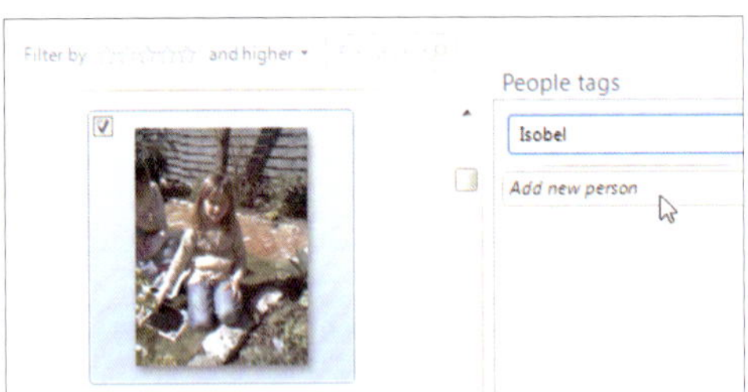

Fig. 3.6 Creating a People Tag

In Photo Gallery you can mark special photos in your collection with 'stars', the range being from 1 to 5 stars, as shown in Fig. 3.7 on the next page.

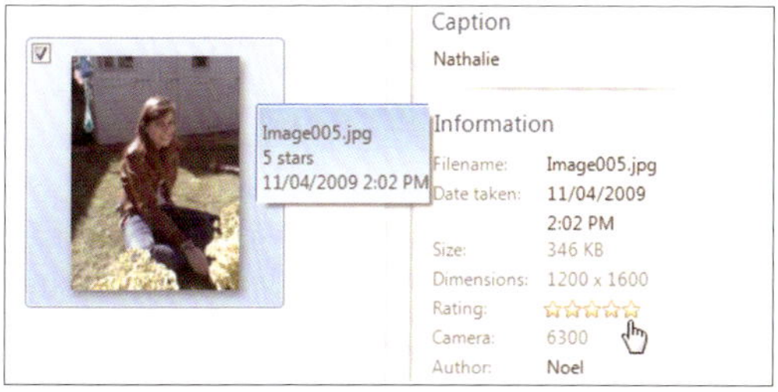

Fig. 3.7 Marking a Selected Photo with Stars

Here we have given a 5 star rating to this special photo by clicking on the 5th star. When next you hover the mouse over the photo, you will see in the pop-up that the photo has been rated correctly with five stars. As seen above, you can add a Caption to the photo and the name of the photographer. In fact, below that you will see additional information about the Exposure, Aperture, and Focal length of the photo, when available.

Searching for Photos

It is no surprise that an application as powerful as Photo Gallery has some very good searching facilities built in. These are found above the thumbnail display area, as shown in Fig. 3.8.

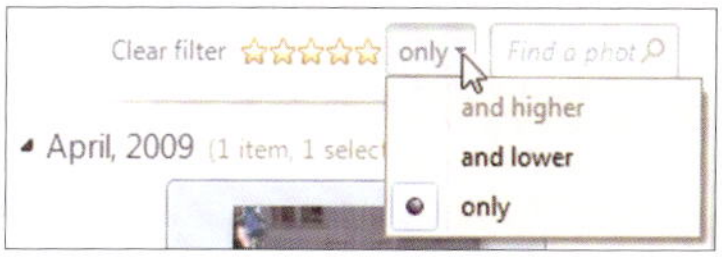

Fig. 3.8 The Photo Filter and Search Options

This shows both the filter and search options. With the filter option you can specify the number of stars you are searching for, and can select further filtering restrictions by clicking the small down-arrow pointed to above, to open the drop-down sub-options shown above.

You can also search for text associated with your photos, including filenames, tags, and captions. You just type your search term in the  Search Box. As you type each letter, the search results change instantly, and the more letters you type the fewer the search results.

Editing and Fixing Photos

When you double-click on the thumbnail of a photo, Photo Gallery opens it in an Editing window where you can fix common problems and create various effects in your photos. Below we show such a photo, opened in the Editing window, in which we have used the **Fix red eye** tool to correct the right eye of the baby. We left the other eye in its original form so you can see how terrible it looks before it is corrected.

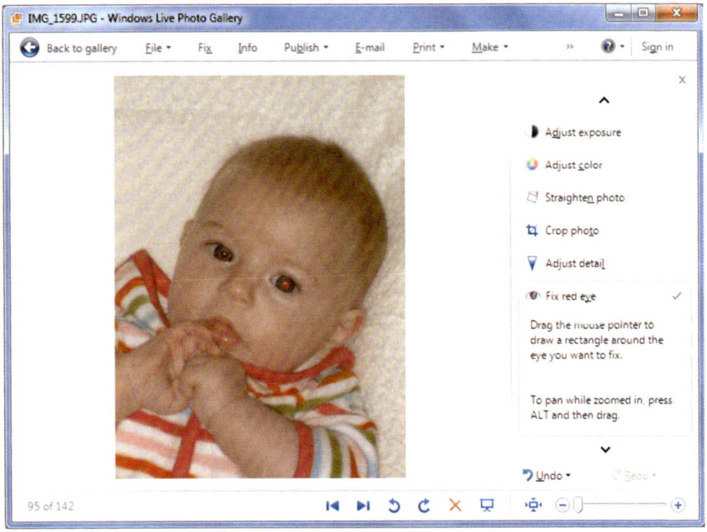

Fig. 3.9 Fixing Red Eye

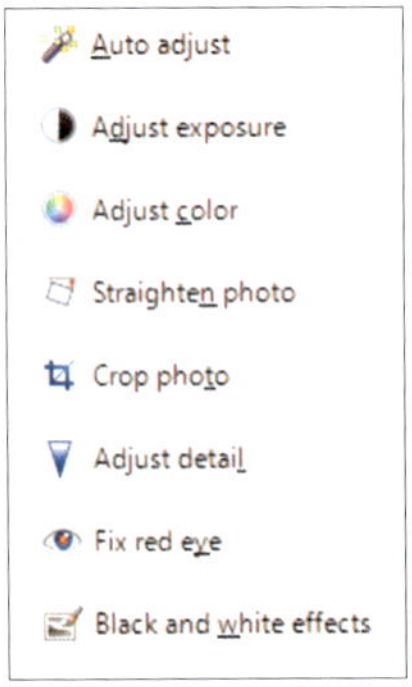

Other basic fixing tools can be used to Auto adjust a photo, Adjust exposure and colour, Straighten and Crop, Adjust detail, and use Black and white effects to enhance your photos.

If you make a mistake, click the 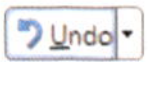 button.

Fig. 3.10 Basic Fixing Tools

Importing from a Camera or Scanner

To import photos and videos from a camera or video recorder or photos from a scanner do the following:

Start Windows Live Photo Gallery, plug in your camera, video recorder or scanner to a USB port of your PC, switch on the appropriate device, then click the **File** menu option to open the sub-menu shown in Fig. 3.11 and click the **Import from a camera or scanner** option.

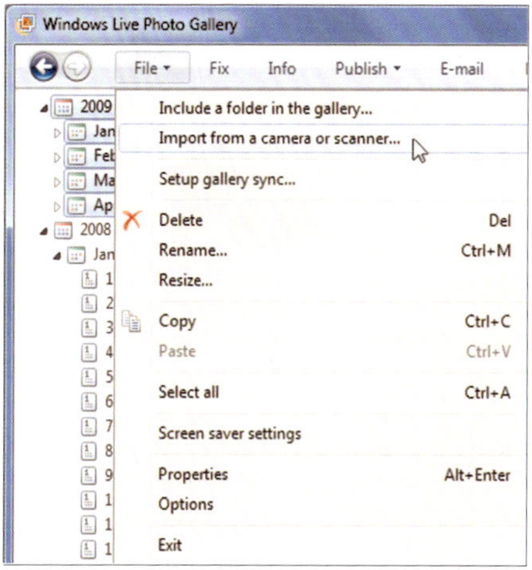

Fig. 3.11 The File Sub-menu Options

We demonstrate the procedure using a camera with which we took a few photographs of a garden. What happens next is shown in Fig. 3.12.

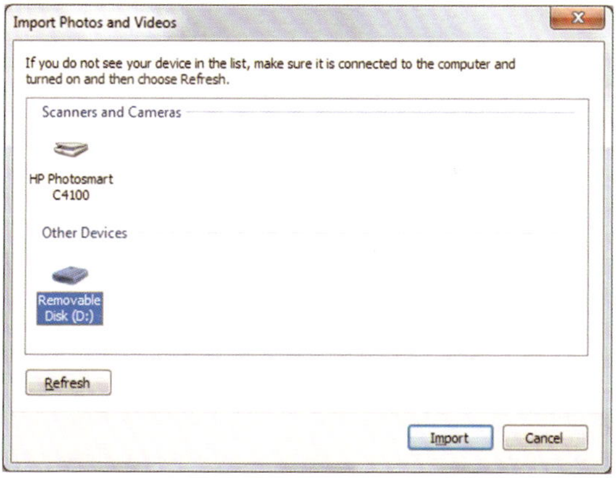

Fig. 3.12 The Scanners, Cameras and Other Devices Box

Our camera, a Sony cyber-shot, is shown as **Removable Disk (D:)** under **Other Devices**, yours could be different. As we also have an HP Photosmart All-in-One Printer/Scanner connected to the PC, Photo Gallery has found it and displayed it under **Scanners and Cameras**.

Now clicking the **Import** button displays the contents of Fig. 3.13.

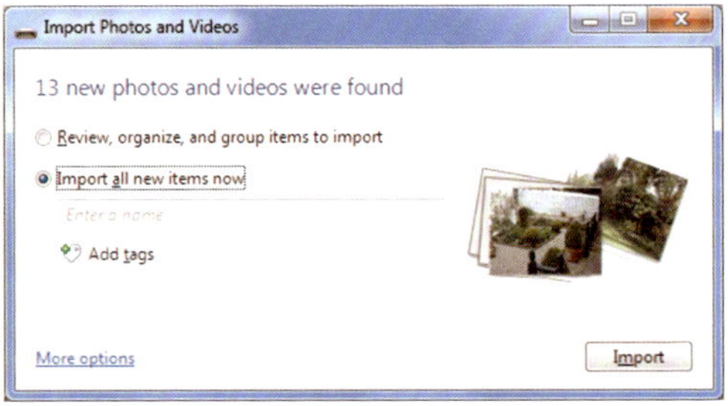

Fig. 3.13 The Import Photos and Videos Dialogue Box

The default option is to **Import all new items now**, and by default the photos are imported into the Pictures folder. However, you can choose the **Review, organize, and group items to import** option, and select in which folder to import, by clicking the appropriate radio button, as shown here.

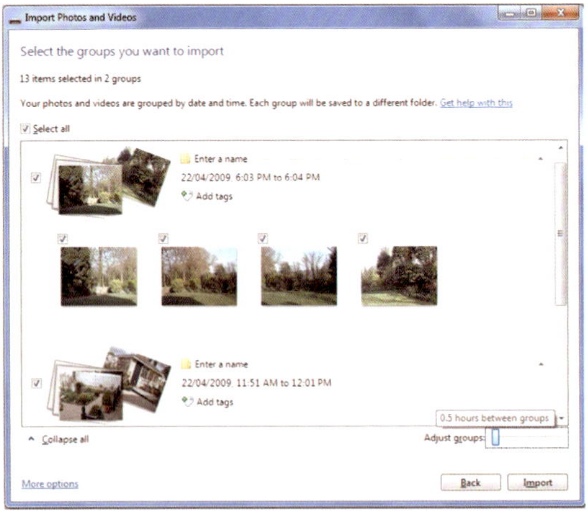

Fig. 3.14 The Import Grouping Dialogue Box

Because we've taken these photos at slightly different times (separated by more than half an hour), they are grouped separately. You could change this grouping time interval with the help of the slider at the bottom-right corner in Fig. 3.14.

Using your Photos

The first thing you'll need to do, after importing photos from a camera or scanner, is to rotate any photos that are not displayed upright, as shown in Fig. 3.15.

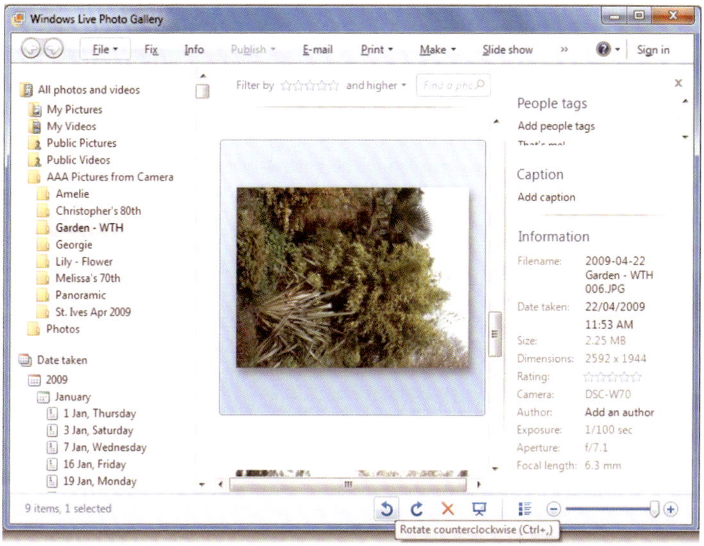

Fig. 3.15 Rotating Photos

To display this photo upright, select it, then click the **Rotate counterclockwise** button at the bottom of the screen. Photos that you don't want to keep can be deleted by selecting each in turn and pressing the **Delete** button.

To see individual details on all the photos in a group next to their thumbnails, click the **View details** button which then changes to the **View thumbnails** button. Clicking it displays the photo thumbnails without the extra information.

Playing a Slide Show

If you want to see all the photos in a group enlarged, the best way is to initiate a slide show by clicking the **Slide Show** button. Whenever the mouse pointer is placed at the bottom of a photo while the **Slide Show** is playing, the following toolbar displays for a while.

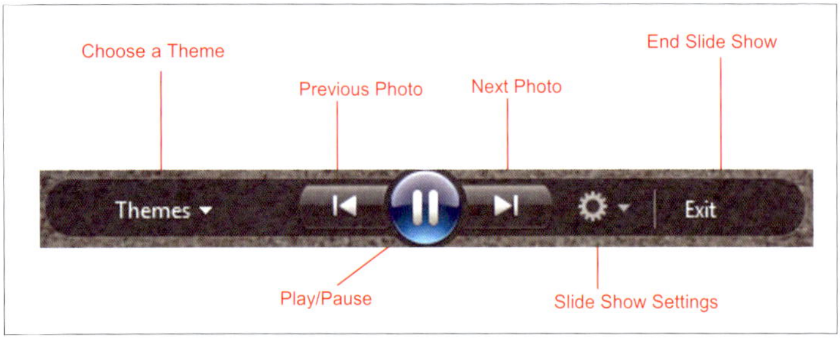

Fig. 3.16 The Slide Show Toolbar

Clicking the Themes toolbar button displays a menu of options for various types of display, including **Pan and zoom**, **Album**, and **Collage**. It is worth spending some time here experimenting with the various options to find out what they do.

Fig. 3.17 Themes

Clicking the toolbar button displays options on how **Fast** or **Slow** the interval between photos is, whether their order is changed, etc., as shown in Fig. 3.18.

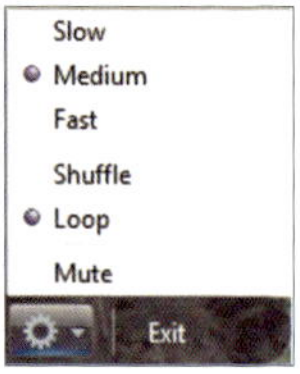

Fig. 3.18

You can stop the **Slide show** at any time by clicking the **Stop** button, which then changes to the **Play** button. Having stopped the **Slide show**, you can then use the left-arrow button to view the previous photo in the group, or the right-arrow button to view the next photo. To restart the **Slide show**, click the **Play** button. To stop and exit the **Slide show**, either click the Exit toolbar button or press the **Esc** keyboard button.

Creating a Panoramic View

Photo Gallery allows you to create a panoramic view out of a set of photos taken for the purpose. To do this, select the photos to be used, click the **Create panoramic photo** sub-menu option of the **Make** menu option, as shown in Fig. 3.19.

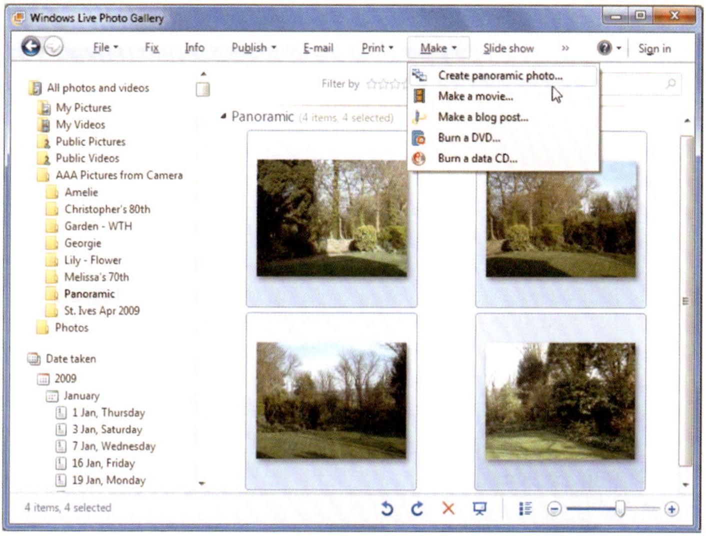

Fig. 3.19 Photos to Create a Panoramic View

A few moments later, Photo Gallery asks you to save the result of its stitching and displays it as shown in Fig. 3.20.

Fig. 3.20 An Automatically Created Panoramic View

If you look closely at the original photos you'll see that the fourth photo does not appear to have been used by the program when creating the panoramic view. We have repeated the process several times with the same result!

Sharing your Photos

Fig. 3.21 shows the three Photo Gallery menu options that can be used to share your photos with others.

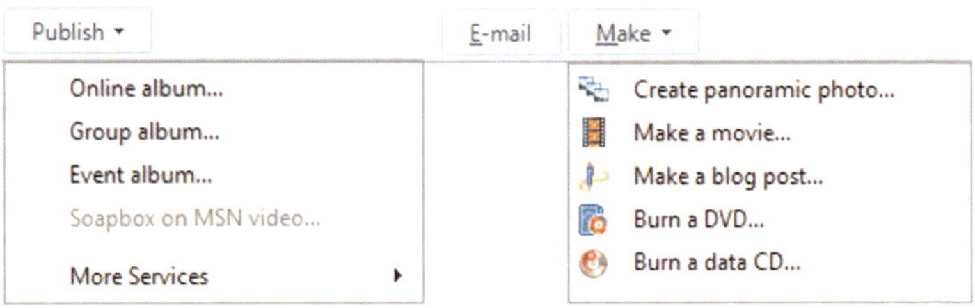

Fig. 3.21 The Publish, E-mail and Make Menu Options

Having organised and edited your photos, you can store them and display them online using one of the **Publish** sub-menu options **Online album**, **Group album**, or **Event album**. With all three options you'll have to first select the photos by holding the **Ctrl** key down while clicking the required photos, before selecting one of the sub-menu options. Windows Live will then ask you to sign in, before you can upload your photos to the Web space allocated to you.

Another method of sharing your photos is to e-mail them as attachments. First select your photos, as described above, then click the **E-mail** menu option which displays a screen asking you to decide on the size of the photos. The larger the photos the longer it will take to send them and receive them at the other end. Once this decision is taken, your e-mail program opens with the photos attached.

The third and final method of sharing photos is to use the **Make** menu option and select one of the sub-menu options; **Make a blog post** (requires you to use the Windows Live Writer to compose your blog before publishing it to popular blogging services), **Burn a DVD**, or **Burn a data CD**. The choice is yours!

4

Windows Live Mail

To be able to communicate electronically with the rest of the world, your PC must be connected to the Internet through some type of modem (usually broadband) to an active phone line. Once this is set up correctly you can send and receive e-mail messages, wherever you are in the World. In this chapter we look at Windows Live Mail, the e-mail program that comes with Windows Live Essentials.

Using Live Mail

Windows Live Mail is Microsoft's excellent all-in-one package for e-mail, contacts management, newsgroups, and feeds. With it you can access several different e-mail accounts from the one window, including Web based accounts from Windows Live Hotmail, MSN Hotmail, AOL, Gmail, and premium Yahoo! Accounts. Its PhotoMail feature lets you easily send large photographs in your messages.

To start Windows Live Mail, click the **Start** button, open the **All Programs** menu, scroll down and click on the Windows Live folder to open it, then click the Windows Live Mail entry. Windows Live Mail then loads entries (if any) from the Windows Calendars, and then asks you if you want to make it your default e-mail program.

As you will probably be using your e-mail program every time you open your PC, perhaps now would be a good time to add it to the **Taskbar** by right-clicking the **Windows Live Mail** entry in the **All Programs** menu and selecting the **Pin to Taskbar** option in the context menu, as shown in Fig. 4.1 on the next page.

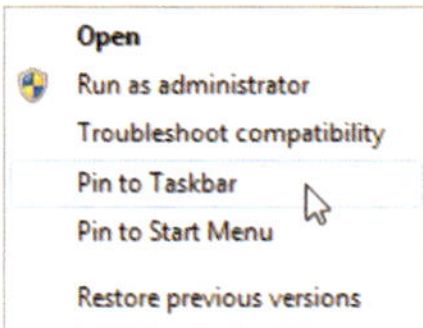

Fig. 4.1
Right-click Menu

An icon is then placed on the right of your Taskbar buttons which can be dragged to where you want it to appear on the bar, as shown below.

Fig. 4.2 Live Mail Icon on Taskbar

Connecting to your Server

When you run Live Mail for the first time, you are prompted to add an e-mail account. You will need the following information from the supplier of your e-mail service: Your e-mail address and password, the type of e-mail server to be used, and the address of the incoming and outgoing e-mail servers you should use.

If the connection process does not start automatically, use the **Tools**, **Accounts** menu command (you might have to first click the **Menus** icon pointed to at the top-right corner of the composite of Fig. 4.3 to display the **Menu** toolbar), click the **Add** button, select **E-mail Account** and click **Next** to start it manually.

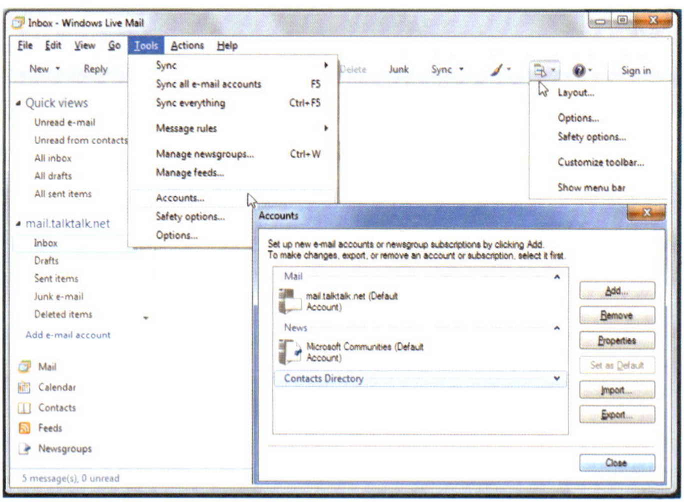

Fig. 4.3 Windows Live Mail Accounts Box

Follow the instructions from screen to screen. It should only take a minute. You can add all your different e-mail accounts like this and view them all from the same window.

Once your connection is established, opening the **Inbox** will display any messages waiting in your mailbox, as shown in Fig. 4.4 below.

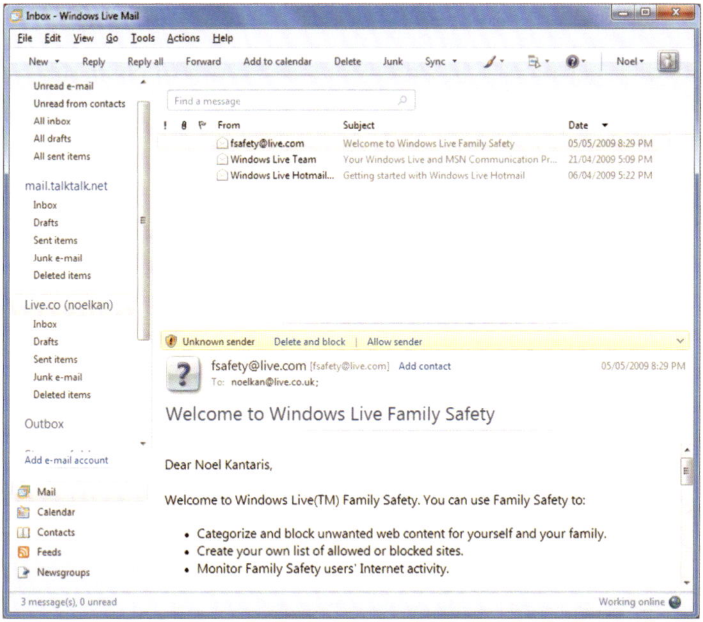

Fig. 4.4 Windows Live Mail Default View

This shows the default layout of the Windows Live Mail window, which consists of the **Folder Pane** on the left, Menu and Tool bars, a **Message List** at the top right pane below the **Find a message** search box, and a **Reading Pane** below the **Message List**.

The **Folder Pane** contains the active mail folders. Clicking on one of these, displays its contents in the **Message List**. Clicking on a message in the list opens a preview of it in the **Reading Pane**, while double-clicking on a message opens the message in its own window.

To check your mail at any time, click the **Sync** toolbar button which with a Broadband connection will automatically download your messages. If you are using a Dial-up connection, it will display the Dial-up Connection window, for you to connect to the Internet. Any new messages will then be downloaded from your mailbox.

Testing your E-mail Settings

Before explaining in more detail the main features of **Windows Live Mail** we will step through the procedure of sending a very simple e-mail message. The best way to test out any unfamiliar e-mail features is to send a test message to your own e-mail address. This saves wasting somebody else's time, and the message can be very quickly checked.

To start, click the **New** button on the toolbar to open the New Message window, shown in Fig. 4.5.

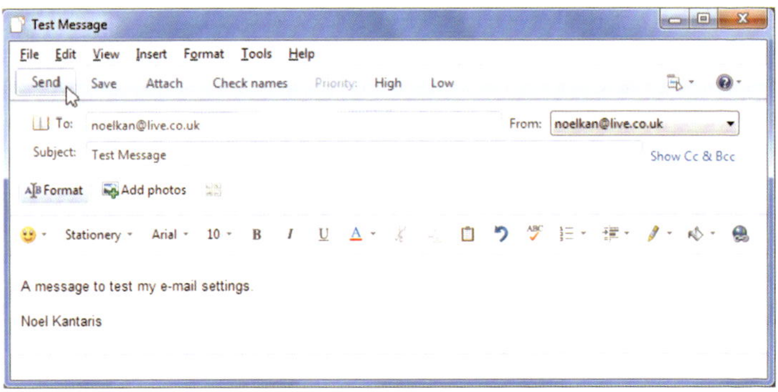

Fig. 4.5 Sending a Test Message

Type your own e-mail address in the **To:** field, and a title for the message in the **Subject:** field. The text in this subject field will form a header for the message when it is received, so it helps to show in a few words what the message is about. Next, type your message in the main body of the window and click the button.

By default, your message is placed in the **Outbox** folder and sent immediately if you are on Broadband, otherwise you will have to press the **Sync** button to send it.

The Main E-mail Window

Windows Live Mail uses three major windows, which we will refer to as: the Main window which opens first; the Read Message window for reading your mail; and the New Message window, to compose your outgoing mail messages.

The Main window consists of a menu, a toolbar, and three panes described next, with the default display shown in our example in Fig. 4.4. You can choose different pane layouts, and customise the toolbar, by clicking the **Menus** button and choosing the **Layout**, or **Customize Toolbar** options, but we will let you try these for yourself.

The Folders List – At the bottom of Fig. 4.6 you see a list of your mail folders with shortcuts to **Mail** , **Calendar** , **Contacts** , **Feeds** and **Newsgroups** . Each account has at least five mail folders, as shown below. If you don't have much space on your screen, you can collapse the 'shortcuts to other features' by clicking the down-arrow (pointed to in Fig. 4.6).

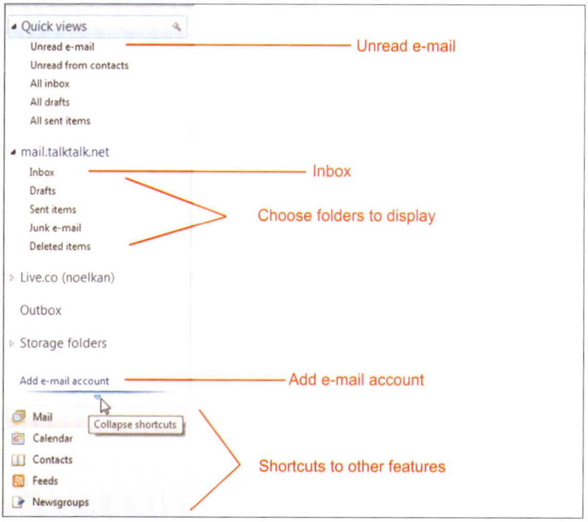

Fig. 4.6 The Default Folders List in Normal View

The **Quick views** option at the top lets you view all the unread mail you have received. This is really useful when you have multiple mail accounts open.

You can add your own folders (usually in the Storage folders section) with the **File**, **Folder**, **Create new folder** command from the Main window. You can then drag messages from the **Message List** and drop them into a folder for storage.

The Message List – When you select a folder, by clicking it in the **Folders List**, the **Message List** shows the contents of that folder with brief details given for each message, as shown here in Fig. 4.7.

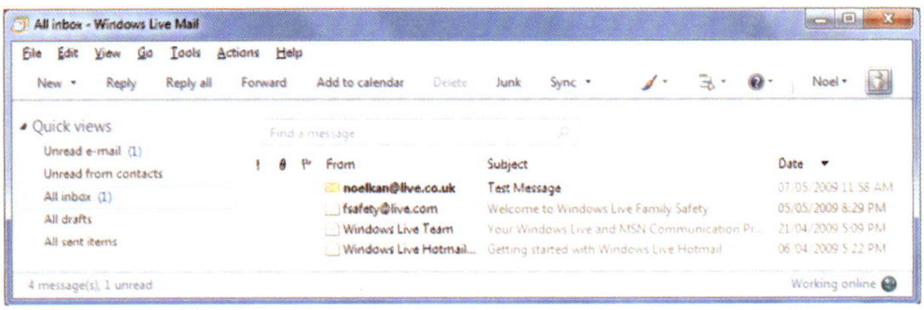

Fig. 4.7 The Message List

The first column shows the message status icons indicating, for example, if a message has an attachment, or has been 'flagged'. The next column shows whether a message has been read, is unread, has been replied to or has been forwarded. Next is the name of the sender, followed by the 'Subject' or title of each message followed, under the **Date** column, the date and time the message was sent.

To sort a list of messages, right-click the **Date** link and choose how you want it sorted from the drop-down menu. You can further control how the message pane displays by clicking the **Menus** button and choosing the **Layout**, **Message List** menu options.

To search for a message term in the list, type the term in the **Find a message** box at the top and click the button.

The Reading Pane – When you select a message in the **Message List**, by clicking it once, it is displayed in the **Reading Pane**, as shown in Fig. 4.4. This lets you read the beginning of the message without actually opening it. If it is worth reading, double-clicking the header in the **Message List**, will open the message in the Read Message window.

The Read Message Window

The Read Message window is shown open in Fig. 4.8 below.

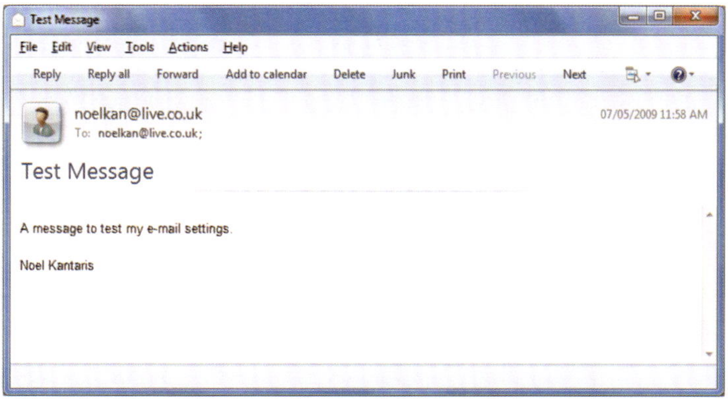

Fig. 4.8 Our Test Message in the Read Message Window

This is the best window to read your mail in. It has its own menu system and self explanatory toolbar, and lets you rapidly process and move between the messages in a folder.

Windows Live Mail has an automated junk filter which scans incoming messages and automatically moves them to the junk folder if it identifies them as spam or a phishing attack. If a message gets through that you don't like, just clicking the **Junk** button will do the same thing. You should make a habit of checking the **Junk e-mail** folder(s) every now and then, as some messages may be put there by mistake. If that happens just clicking the **Not junk** button will move the message to your **Inbox**.

The New Message Window

Clicking the **New** button New on the Main Window toolbar opens the New Message window. This is where you create your e-mail messages in Live Mail and it is important to understand its features, so that you can get the most out of it.

The toolbar icons in this window are all self explanatory, but if necessary, hovering the pointer over one will tell you what it does. Also have a look at the message itself in Fig. 4.9 for additional explanations.

Message Formatting

Windows Live Mail provides quite sophisticated formatting options from both the **Format** menu and the Format toolbar. These only work if you prepare the message in HTML format, as used in Web documents. You can set this to be your default mail sending format using the Send tab in the **Tools**, **Options** box of the **Main Window**.

The **Format** toolbar, shown open in Fig. 4.9, is added to the New Message window when you are in HTML mode and all the **Format** menu options are then made active.

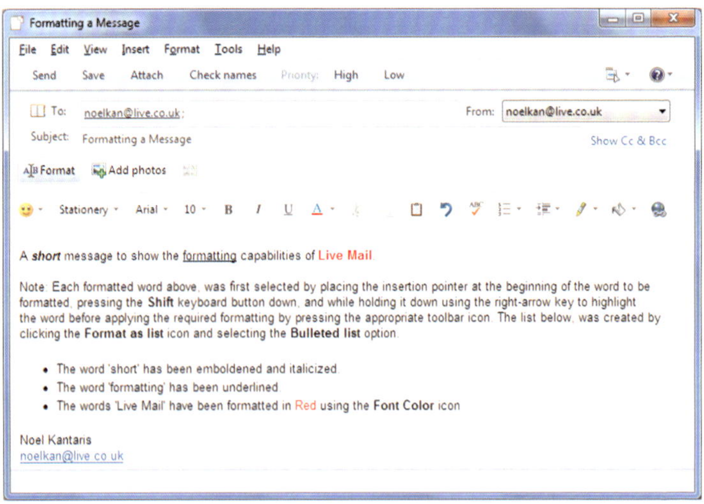

Fig. 4.9 The New Message Window

Photo E-mail

You can add photos to e-mail messages in two ways, as attachments (described on the next page), or in a photo e-mail. With a photo e-mail, as long as you are signed in to Windows Live Mail with a Windows Live ID, you can upload the full versions of your photos and save them on Windows' servers. Only thumbnails of them will be placed in your message, so your e-mail will be smaller and quicker to send, but the recipient will be able to view or download the full photos.

To create a photo e-mail, click the **New** button New to open the New Message window, shown in Fig. 4.10, and prepare your message as normal. Click where you want to insert photos in the message and then click the **Add photos** button Add photos. Select the photos you want to send followed by the **Add** button, and click **Done** to finish.

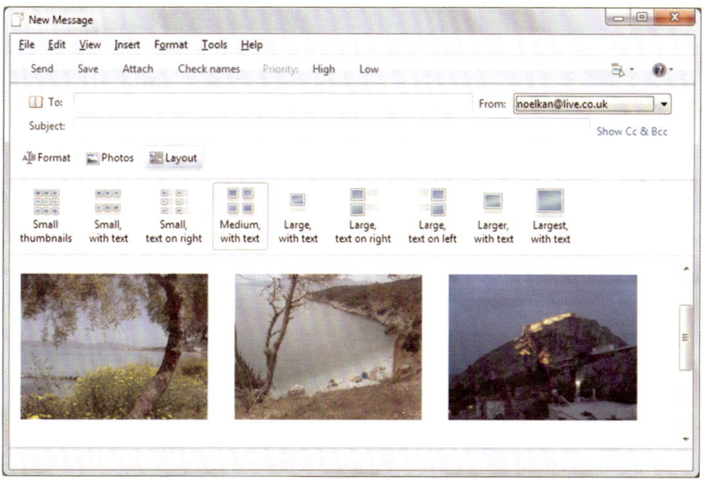

Fig. 4.10 Thumbnails in a Photo E-mail

To format your message, you click Format to format the text, Photos to add photo frames or more photos, and Layout to set the message layout, as shown in Fig. 4.10 above. Finally click the **Send** button to send your Photo e-mail. This really is well worth doing.

E-mail Attachments

To add an attachment to an e-mail message, such as a photo or another type of file, you simply click the **Attach** button 

in the New Message window, select the file(s), you want to send with your message, and click **Open**.

In **Windows Live Mail** the attached files are placed below the **Subject** box. In Fig. 4.11 we show two attachments with their icons telling the recipient what each file is; a graphics (**.jpg**) file, and a text (**.txt**) file in this case. Finally clicking the **Send** button, sends the e-mail to the recipient(s).

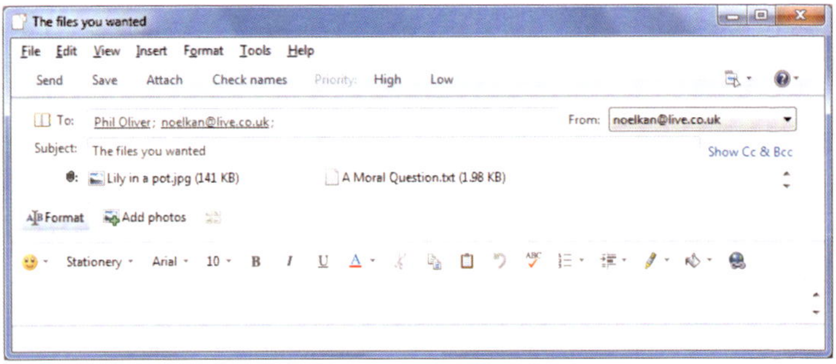

Fig. 4.11 A New E-mail with two Attachments

Receiving Attachments

Fig. 4.12, on the next page, shows the received e-mail with the two attachments in a Read Message window. The received message shows the graphics (**.jpg**) file open at the bottom of the window, and both attachments in the Header bar with icons indicating what type of files they are.

Right-clicking an attachment opens a drop-down menu also shown in Fig. 4.12. From this you can choose to open, print or save the attached files. The **Save all** option is the one most often used.

Double-clicking an attached file icon opens a Mail Attachment window showing you the type of document and asking whether you want to open it. A graphics file (**.jpg**) then opens in **Windows Live Photo Gallery**, and a Word document file opens in Microsoft Word.

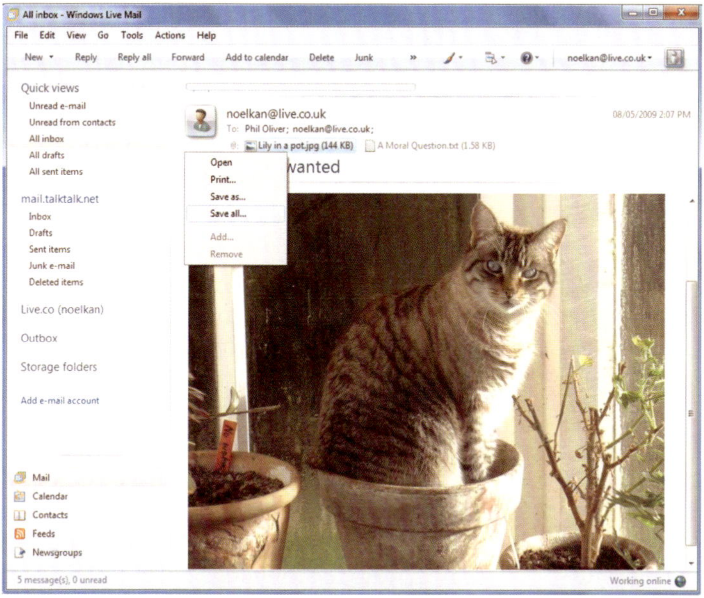

Fig. 4.12 Received Attachments in a Read Message Window

As long as you have the necessary programs, each attached file can be opened in situ or saved to disc from within the application that opened it.

Replying to a Message

When you receive an e-mail message that you want to reply to, simply click the **Reply** button Reply to open the New Message window. The reply address and the subject field are both filled in automatically for you, and the text of the message you are replying to will, by default, be placed under the insertion point.

You can edit this text, so that it is obvious what you are referring to. Just a few lines may well be enough. Then type your reply, format whatever you want and click the **Send** button Send.

Deleting Messages

Some e-mail messages you receive will be worth keeping, but most will need deleting. To do this, just click the **Delete** button 

on the Read Message window. From the Main window you can select the messages you don't want to keep in the **Messages List** and either, click the **Delete** button 

, or press the **Delete** keyboard key.

Whenever you delete a message it is actually moved to the **Deleted Items** folder. If ignored, this folder gets bigger and bigger over time, so you need to check it frequently and manually re-delete messages you will not need again.

To get this done automatically, you use the **Tools**, **Options** menu command to open the Options dialogue box, click the Advanced tab and click the **Maintenance** button at the bottom of the screen and check the **Empty messages from the 'Deleted Items' folder on exit** box in the displayed Maintenance screen. Your deletions will then be automatically removed whenever you close Live Mail.

Spell Checking Messages

Just because e-mail messages are a quick way of getting in touch with friends and family, there is no reason why they should be full of spelling mistakes, as Windows Live Mail has a good spelling checker built in.

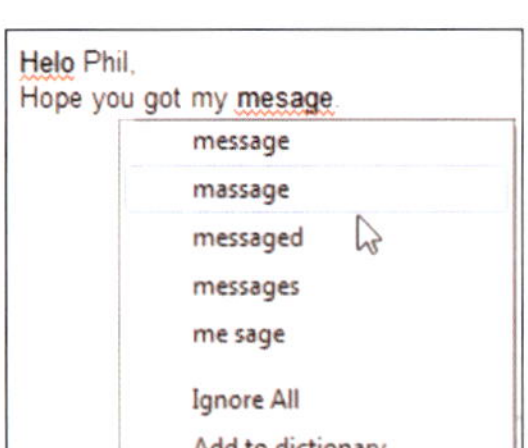

Fig. 4.13 Correcting Spelling Mistakes

To try it out, prepare a message in the New Message window, but with obvious spelling mistakes. Errors will be underlined in red, as shown in Fig. 4.13.

Right-clicking a flagged 'error' opens a drop-down menu. You can accept a suggestion, **Ignore All** occurrences, or add your original word to the dictionary for future use. This works very well.

Organising your Messages

As we saw earlier in this chapter, you can open folders or create your own folders, and also you can drag messages to move them from one folder into another. The copy procedure is the same, except you must also have the **Ctrl** key depressed through the dragging procedure.

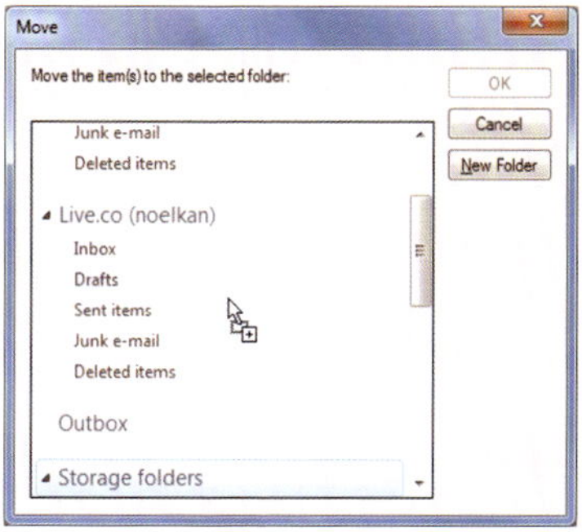

Fig. 4.14 Moving a Message

You can tell that copying is taking place by the '+' on the mouse pointer as shown here to the right and in Fig. 4.14.

The System Folders

Windows Live Mail has six folders which it always keeps intact and will not let you delete. These are:

- The **Inbox** folder holds all incoming messages; you should delete or move them from this folder as soon as you have read them. Messages in the **Inbox** folder can be moved or copied into any other folder except the **Outbox** folder.
- The **Outbox** folder holds messages that have been prepared but not yet transmitted. As soon as the messages are sent they are automatically removed to the **Sent Items** folder. Messages in the **Outbox** folder can be moved or copied into any of the other folders.
- The **Sent Items** folder holds messages that have been transmitted. You can then 'file' copies of these messages, or delete them. Messages in the **Sent Items** folder can be moved or copied into any of the other folders except the **Outbox** folder.

- The **Deleted Items** folder holds messages that have been deleted and placed in there as a safety feature. Messages in the **Deleted Items** folder can be moved or copied into any of the other folders, except the **Outbox** folder.
- The **Drafts** folder is used to hold a message you closed down without sending by selecting the **File**, **Send Later** menu command. A Message in the **Drafts** folder cannot be moved or copied into any other folder. Simply double-click it to open it in its own window, edit it, and click the **Send** button.

Getting Help in Live Mail

As you would expect, Live Mail has a **Help** system which you can activate whenever you want. It is opened by either clicking the **Help** button, or clicking the **Help** Menu bar option. Either one of these opens the drop-down menu shown in Fig. 4.15.

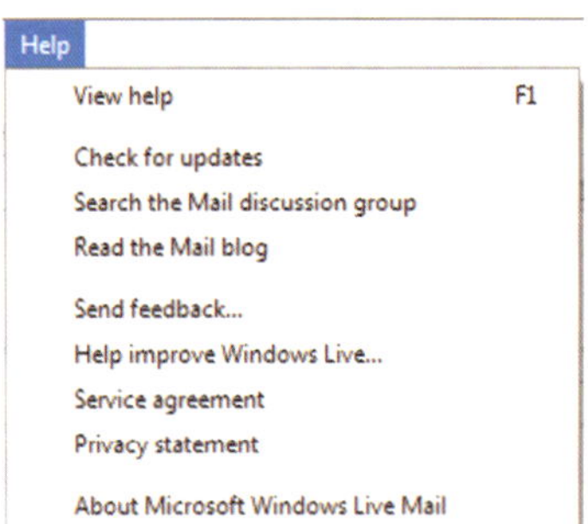

Fig. 4.15 The Help Menu.

Selecting **View Help** from the drop-down menu, or pressing the **F1** button when in any of the Windows Live screens, opens an Explorer screen and displays a vast amount of information.

We suggest you spend some time getting familiar with this Help system, which should answer most of your future queries. Good luck!

* * *

In the next chapter we will cover additional Features of Live Mail, such as Calendar, RSS feeds, and Newsgroups.

5

Other Live Mail Features

Windows Live Mail includes additional features which are extremely useful, so we will be covering these in this chapter.

The Contacts List

Windows Live Mail lets you create and keep a contact list to store details such as the names, addresses, phone numbers, and e-mail addresses of your contacts.

If you have never signed in to Live Mail with a Windows Live ID, your contact list will contain only the contacts you have added or imported into the program. If you are signed in, Live Mail uses the contact list associated with your Windows Live ID and any changes that you make to your contacts in Live Mail will be saved and also used in Windows Live Messenger, Windows Live Hotmail, and other Live services.

In Live Mail you click the **Contacts** button at the bottom of the **Folder Pane** to access the **Contacts** window.

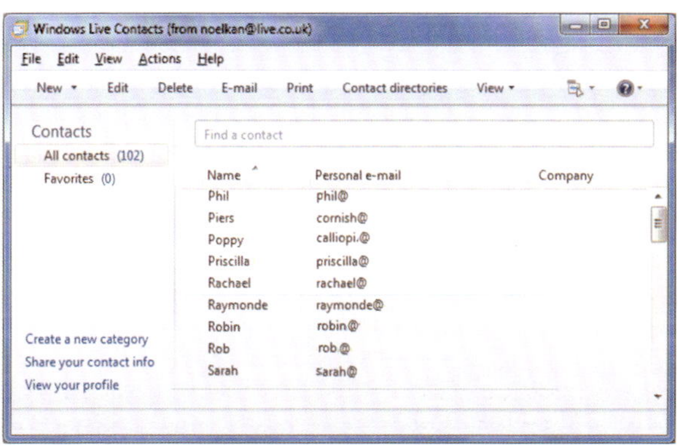

Fig. 5.1 The Live Mail Contacts Window

In Fig. 5.1 on the previous page, we show a small part our **Contacts** list in default view. However, to preserve anonymity we have obscured the surname and part of each person's e-mail address. Different views of the Contacts window can be displayed by clicking the **View** button View ▾ and selecting an option.

You can add a person's details in the **Add a Contact** box opened by clicking the **New** button New ▾, as shown in Fig. 5.2 below.

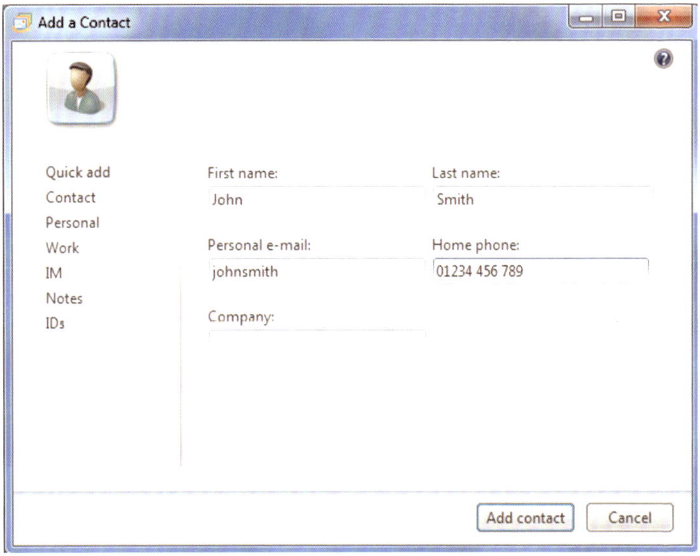

Fig. 5.2 The Add a Contact Window

Use the Quick or Contact option screen to enter the name, phone, and e-mail details for your new contact. The Personal option screen is used to enter their personal address, phone and fax numbers, and Web site. You can also enter similar information for Work. The rest of the information can be entered if you have the time, or be entered later by editing the Contact's entry.

Unfortunately, there does not seem to be any facility for adding photos of your contacts, as in earlier versions.

To send a new message from your **Contacts** list, highlight their name and click the **E-mail** button E-mail to open a pre-addressed New Message window in Live Mail.

Alternatively, use the New Message window, start typing a name in the To: box and select from the options presented, or click on the To: button, or use the **Actions**, **Send e-mail** command, to open the box Shown in Fig. 5.3 below.

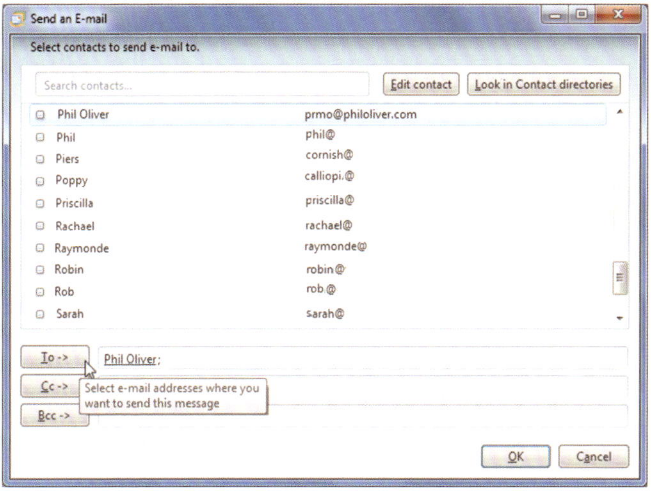

Fig. 5.3 Selecting a Contact

In this box, you can select a person's name and click either the **To:** button, pointed to above, to place it in the **To** field of your message, the **Cc:** button to place it in the **Copy** field, or the **Bcc:** button to place it in the **Blind Copy** field.

The **Bcc** field is used if you do not want the address entered there to be visible to the main recipient of the message.

The Windows Calendar

Windows Live Mail also provides you with a calendar which is opened by clicking the **Calendar** button at the bottom of the **Folder Pane**.

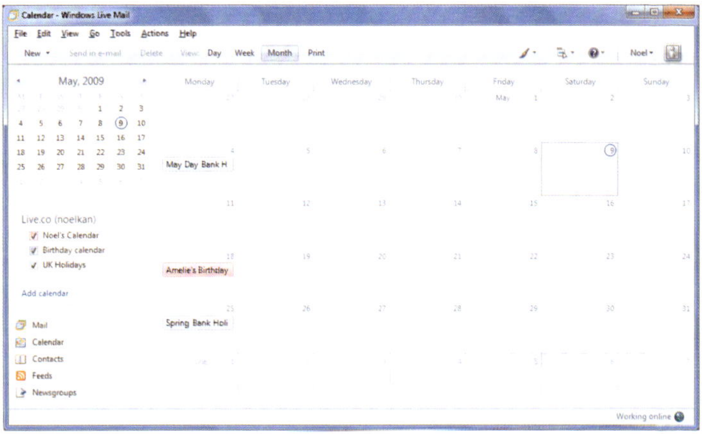

Fig. 5.4 The Live Mail Calendar

This provides you with all the scheduling tools you should ever need. Windows Live Calendar provides day, week and month views, and supports multiple, colour-coded calendars, making it easy to keep schedules for work, family, school, etc. Also note that certain information was transferred from our previous calendar and is shown above.

Changing the month you are viewing could not be simpler; just click the scroll buttons on either side of the currently displaying month – clicking the left button displays earlier months, while clicking the right button displays later months (see also Fig. 5.5 on the next page).

To see the Calendar in daily or weekly view, simply click the appropriate button on the Calendar toolbar, shown below

or use the **View** command, then select **Day** or **Week** from the drop-down menu.

Viewing Appointments

All the details of appointments, events or meetings can be viewed in Calendar whether you are in the Daily, Weekly, or Monthly view; you can see the date, and the description. In Weekly and Daily view you can also see the time of an appointment and the ⟳ symbol to indicate that the appointment is recurring. In Fig. 5.5 below, the Calendar is displayed in Weekly View.

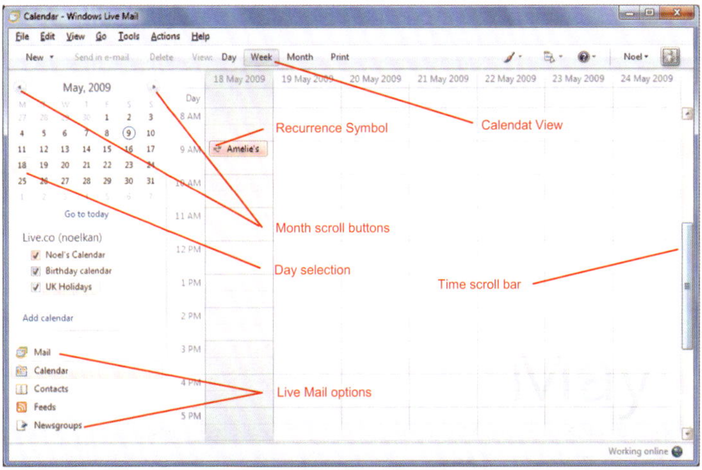

Fig. 5.5 The Calendar Display in Weekly View

The Calendar List

To the left of the Calendar screen you'll see a list of calendars; three in our case.

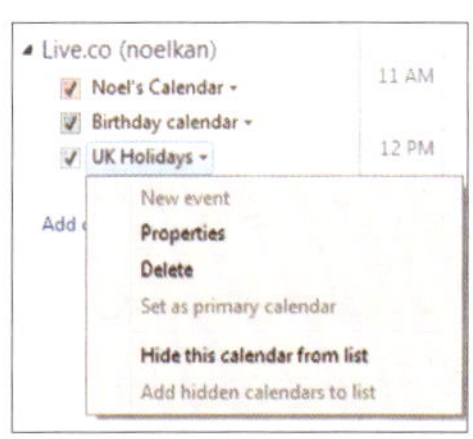

Fig. 5.6 Calendar List

- The 'Primary Calendar' appears at the top of the list and contains all the information appearing within the rest of the calendars on the list.
- The 'Birthday Calendar' contains all the birthdays of your Contacts, provided you have entered that information in the Contacts list.

- The 'UK Holidays' calendar contains all the holidays in the UK.

Clicking any of these calendars displays the drop-down menu shown in Fig. 5.6. The **Properties** option allows you to select the colour that events display in that specific calendar.

Entering Events

As an example we will now create a recurring event in the Primary Calendar to, say, meet Section Managers, that takes place on Wednesday every four weeks starting at 10:00 a.m., on 20 May and lasts for 2 hours.

To do so in the **Day View**, click on 20 May on the calendar to the left of the entry area, move the cursor to 10:00 a.m., and either right-click or click the **Actions** menu option and select **New event** from the drop-down sub-menu. This opens the New Event dialogue box displayed in Fig. 5.7 below.

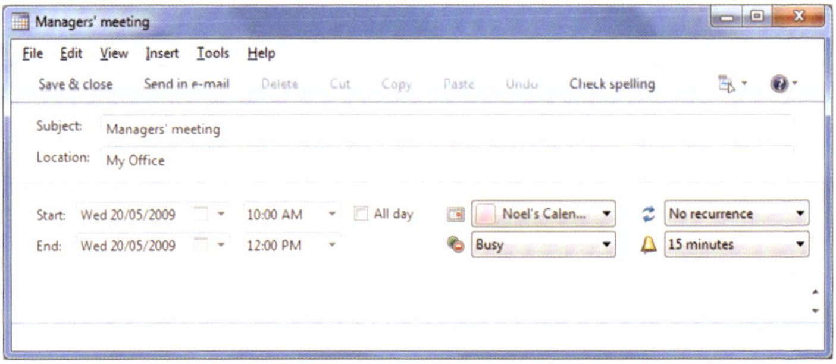

Fig. 5.7 The New Event Dialogue Box

The same dialogue box opens if you double-click the time box of the specified day.

In this dialogue box, type 'Managers' meeting' in the **Subject** box, and 'My Office' in the **Location** box, and set the **End time** to 12.00, as shown in Fig. 5.7 above.

Next, click the **Reminder** button and select 15 minutes, then click the **Recurrence** button and select **Custom** from the drop-down menu to open the Event Recurrence box shown in Fig. 5.8 on the next page.

Click the **Weekly** button and in the **Every** box, type '4', and tick the **Wednesday** box, as shown in Fig. 5.8, then click **OK**. Finally, click the **Save & Close** button located at the top of the first dialogue box.

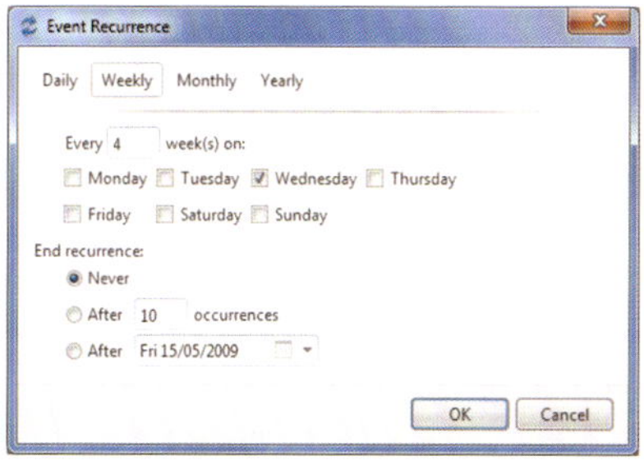

Fig. 5.8 The Event Recurrence Box

Information relevant to an appointment or meeting is now displayed in the Calendar, including the Recurrence symbol and location (the latter only appears in the **Daily** and **Weekly** Views). Hovering the mouse pointer over an event, shows additional detail, as in Fig. 5.9.

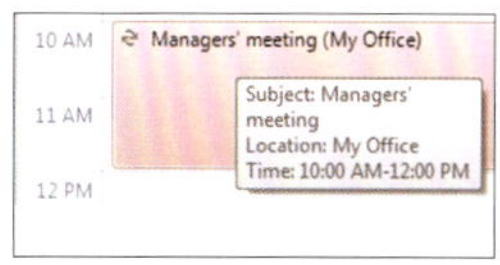

Fig. 5.9 Additional

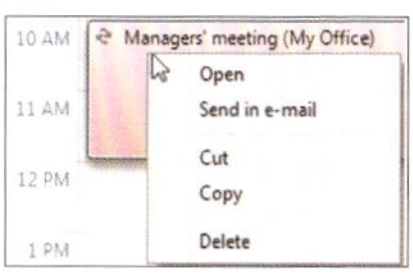

Fig. 5.10 Event Menu

If you want to make any changes to the newly created appointment, point to it and right-click it. You can use the options on this drop-down menu (Fig. 5.10) to send it in an e-mail, to open it, to edit it, or delete it.

Selecting to **Open** the event, displays an additional box, shown in Fig. 5.11, asking you whether you want to **Edit this occurrence** or **Edit all occurrences**. Choosing the **Edit all occurrences** option, opens the Event Recurrence box where you can make the required changes.

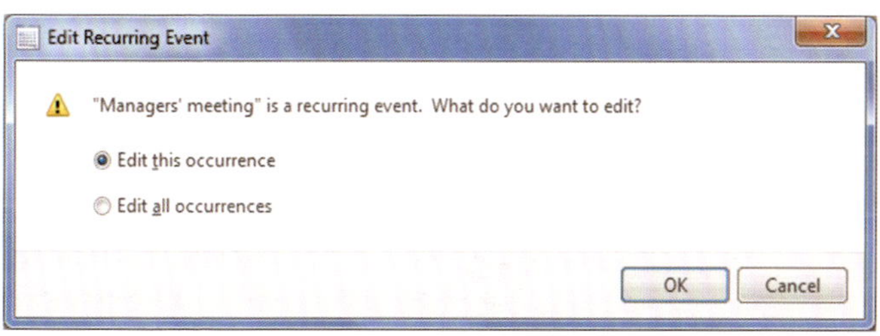

Fig. 5.11 Editing a Recurring Event

Next, let us now assume that you also have a special lunch appointment with your mother on the 17th of June each year, as it is her birthday. To enter this event, click on 17 June on the calendar to the left of the Daily entry area, and create a yearly event 'Lunch with mother' for 1:00 p.m., for 1½ hours. We have added 'Birthday Lunch' in Location to distinguish it from other types of lunches, as shown in Fig. 5.12 below.

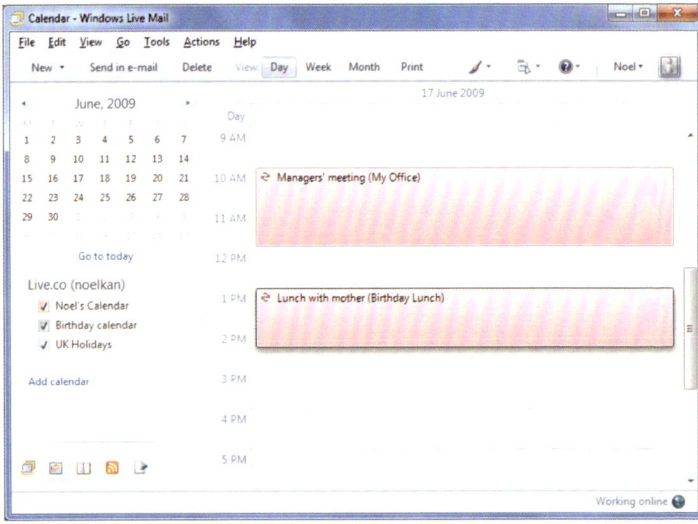

Fig. 5.12 Entering a Yearly Appointment.

Note that the meeting with the Managers is also shown on the same day, as it is four weeks since the last meeting. This information also appears on the Weekly and the Monthly view, except that on the Monthly view you get a somewhat restricted display of your appointments, as shown here in Fig. 5.13, even though the Monthly display was maximised on the screen. Try it!

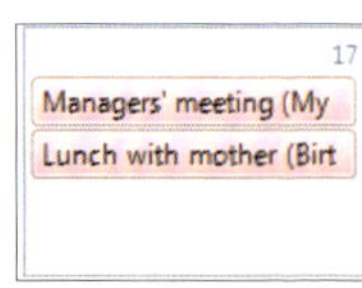

Fig. 5.13 Monthly View

Planning a Meeting

Suppose we decide to invite other people into the meeting with the Managers on 17 June. First, locate the date of the meeting on the Calendar display and double-click the entry in question.

In the displayed 'Edit Recurring Event' screen, click the **Edit this occurrence** radio button to display the Managers' meeting dialogue box, then click the **Send in e-mail** button 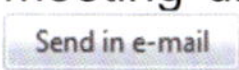

to obtain the screen in Fig. 5.14, in which you include the e-mail addresses of the colleague(s) you would like to be present at the meeting. Next, type in the main body of the e-mail something similar to our one line 'You are invited ...' (you can, of course, type more lines if you want).

The rest of the information (subject line, and details of the meeting below our one-line message), were automatically inserted by Calendar. This really saves time and effort – it could not be easier!

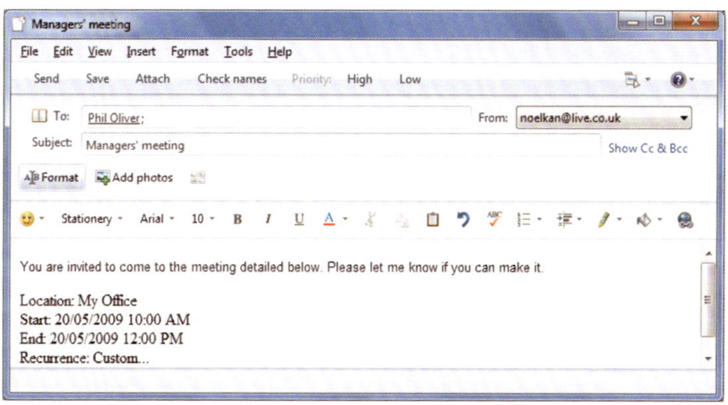

Fig. 5.14 Scheduling Colleagues to Attend a Meeting

From here, you can organise meetings and send requests to participants and then track the status of their response provided, of course, you are either connected to a local network or know their e-mail address.

Using RSS Feeds

With Windows Live Mail, you can now read and manage your blogs and RSS feeds from within the application, at the same time as handling your e-mail and calendar.

RSS stands for 'Really Simple Syndication'. They are also called 'Feeds' and are just Web pages, designed to be read by computers rather than people. RSS is a way for publishers of online news agencies and magazines to make news, blogs, and other content freely available to subscribers. You find what you want, subscribe to it, and then every time the author updates the content or writes something new, it is delivered straight to Live Mail on your desk. Feeds offer an easy way to keep up to date with what you are interested in.

The usual way to find a new RSS feed is to look on your favourite Web sites and if they offer this feature, you will see the icon. Clicking such an icon will open a Feed page. If you like it, look for the link that lets you 'subscribe' and click it, as shown in Fig. 5.15.

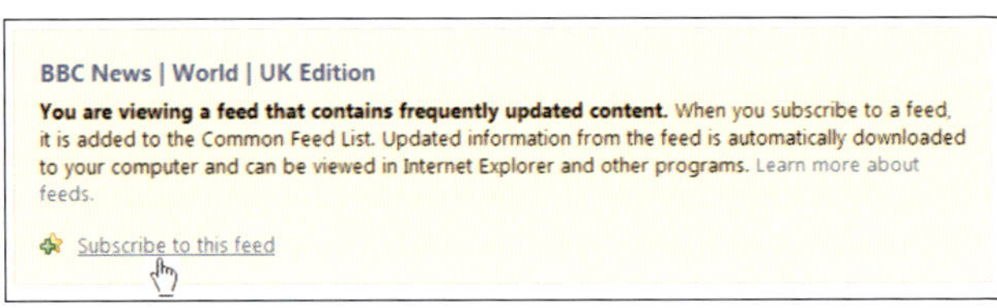

Fig. 5.15 Subscribing to a Feed Using Explorer

This opens the Subscribe to this Feed dialogue box, as shown in Fig. 5.16. Clicking the **Subscribe** button completes the procedure. Next time you open Windows Live Mail and click on the Feed button your newly created feed will be there, as shown in Fig. 5.17 on the next page.

Fig. 5.16 The Subscribe to a Feed Box

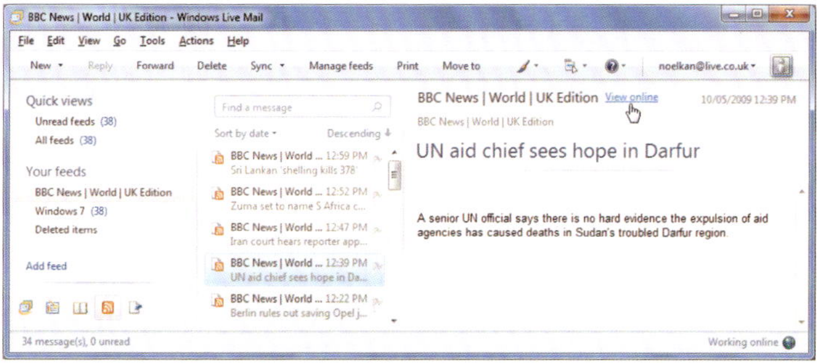

Fig. 5.17 Reading a Feed

When you select a Feed, its downloaded contents are displayed, as shown above. Live Mail checks the RSS publisher's server for new and updated items on a regular basis.

You can open a selected Feed by clicking on the **View on line** link, pointed to above, which launches Internet Explorer and displays the full article in it, as shown in Fig. 5.18.

Fig. 5.18 A Feed Message Opened in Internet Explorer

To delete a Feed, or a specific Feed message, select the Feed or the Feed message, and click the **Delete** button Delete. You need to keep an eye on Feed messages because they can build up rather quickly!

You can update Feed messages instantly by pressing the **Sync** button Sync, manage feeds or move them by pressing the corresponding toolbar buttons. It is worth getting to know the RSS Feeds facility. Try it!

Using Newsgroups

You can use Windows Live Mail to get in touch with Newsgroups. Newsgroups are similar to the public message boards of old, and are used to focus on a particular topic of interest to its readers. There are currently well over 100,000 Usenet newsgroups, but only a quarter or so of those are active.

Newsgroups vary in popularity, with some only getting a few posts a month while others get several hundred or more messages a day. Newsgroups normally have administrators who decide how long articles are kept on their server before being deleted; some may keep articles for as little as one or two weeks, others may hold them for many months particularly if the articles deal with technical matters.

To start the application click the Newsgroups icon at the bottom of the Live Mail screen to open the screen shown in Fig. 5.19 with the Microsoft Communities option to the left, selected.

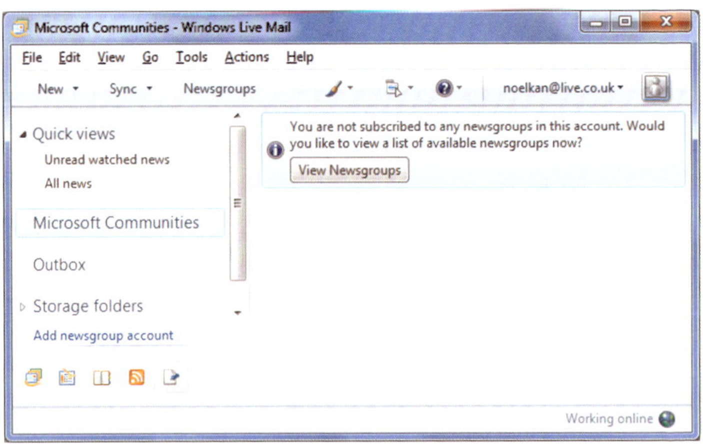

Fig. 5.19 Microsoft Communities

Clicking the **View Newsgroups** button displays a screen similar to the one shown in Fig. 5.20 on the next page, with several hundred entries of interest.

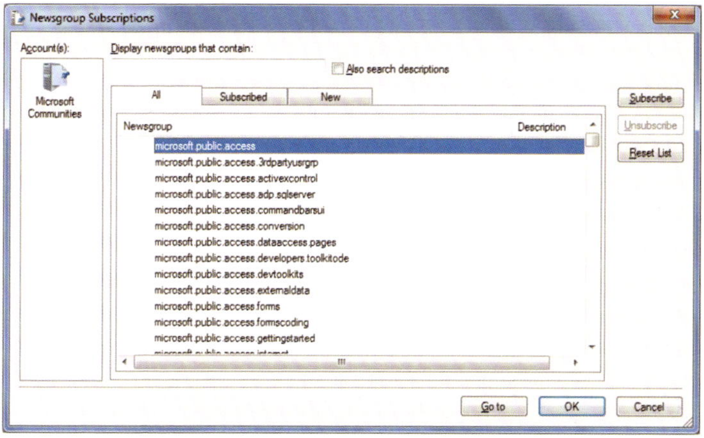

Fig. 5.20 Microsoft Newsgroups Sites

You can search for topics contained in these Newsgroups by typing something similar to what we show below. We are naturally interested in the subject of Windows Live, so that is what we typed. This narrows down the available sites to one in our case, as shown below.

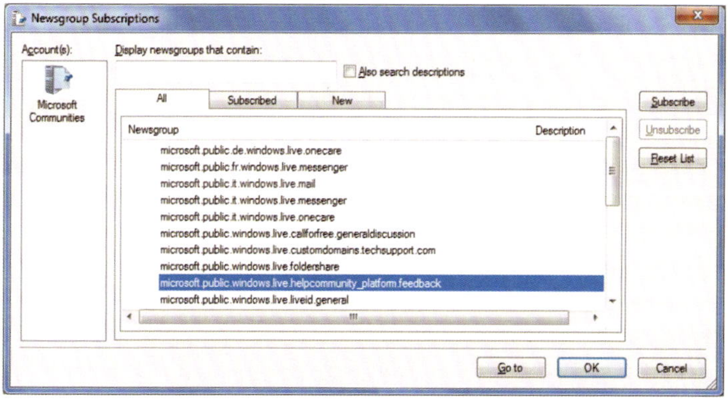

Fig. 5.21 The Microsoft Windows Live Subgroups

Note that the list above includes abbreviations such as de (for German), fr (for French), it (for Italian) sites. We selected one without such abbreviations in its name and clicked the **Go to** button. The screen that opened for us is shown in Fig. 5.22 on the next page.

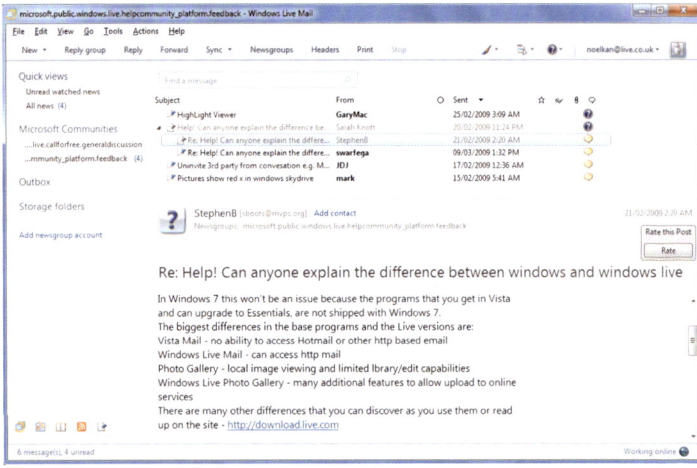

Fig. 5.22 An Answer to a Query Posted on a Windows Live Newsgroup

Note that if a query has been answered, a horizontal arrowhead ▷ appears against the original message. Clicking this symbol opens all the answers relating to the query and the symbol now changes to an inclined arrowhead ◢, as it is also shown in Fig. 5.22 above.

You can rate an answer, if you so wish, or answer the person who posted the question directly by clicking the **Reply** menu button and sending your answer via e-mail, or posting it for everyone in the Newsgroup to see by clicking the **Reply group** menu button which displays the group answer box ready for you to type your message.

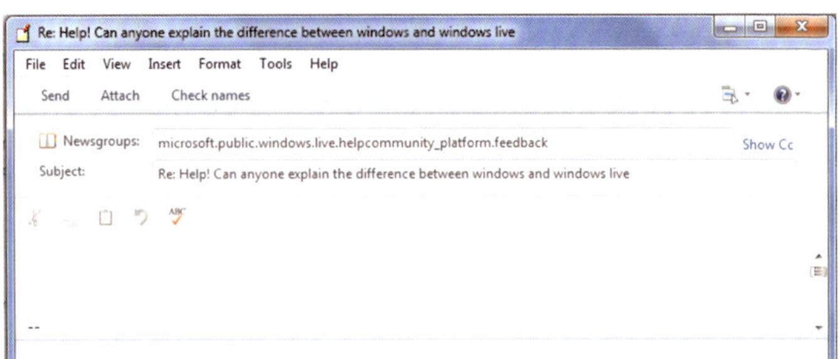

Fig. 5.23 Posting a Reply to a Group

6

Windows Live Writer

Windows Live Writer is used to create and format short online newsletters (blogs – short for Weblogs) that are frequently updated and are available for the general public to read.

Blogs are generally text posts, but a lot of them these days include rich content, such as images, maps, tables, hyperlinks (that provide links to other blogs, Web pages and other media with the same topic), and tags (keywords that can be assigned to a blog post to indicate the category of the blog). The ability for readers to leave comments in an interactive format is an important part of any blog. Windows Live Writer makes these facilities very easy to use.

If you want to see an explanation of what a blog is in plain English, then have a look at the YouTube link below:

www.commoncraft.com/blogs

and start the video to display what is shown here in Fig. 6.1 after a few seconds.

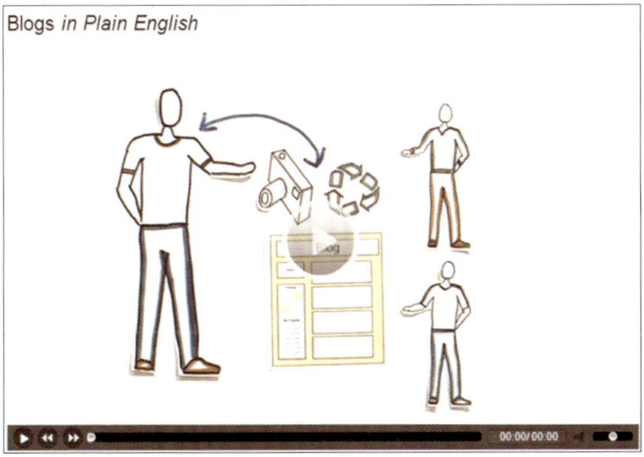

Fig. 6.1 A Good Explanation of Blogging

Before we look at Windows Live Writer in some detail, it might be a good idea to have a look at existing blogs on the Internet. By now there are around 70 million blog sites on various subjects and to find the one you are interested in might be a rather daunting experience. Various search engines make this easier for you, the most popular being Google. Start your Web browser and type in the address box:

www.blogsearch.google.com

to open the screen shown in Fig. 6.2 below.

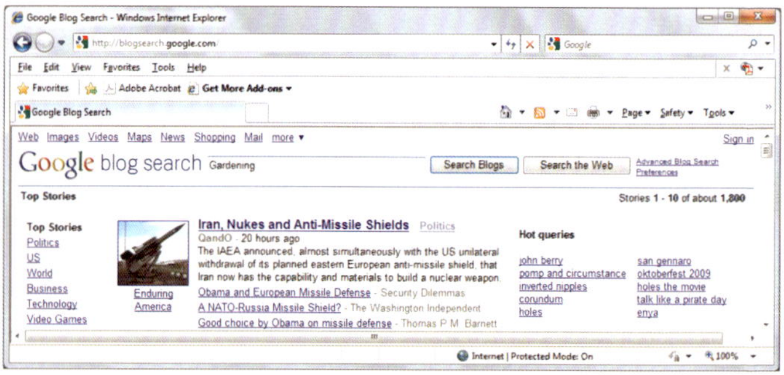

Fig. 6.2 The Google Blog Search Screen

Next, type in the Search box what you are looking for, say 'Gardening', to open a screen similar to that in Fig. 6.3.

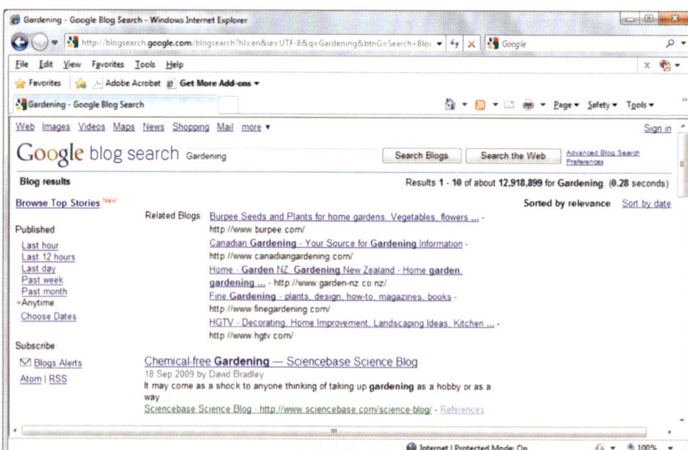

Fig. 6.3 Some of the Available Blog Sites on Gardening

As you can see, there are nearly 13 million blog sites on this subject alone! Have a look at some to see what people write about and how they structure their blogs.

Using Live Writer to Create a Blog

Live Writer can be used in two ways to create your blog. The first method is to create a blog post from an existing Website, while the second is to create a blog from scratch. We shall examine each of these separately.

Creating a Blog from an Existing Web Site

Start Windows Internet Explorer and navigate to the Web site page that contains the information you want to include in your blog. We chose here to use one of our Websites that contains a list of our books, as shown below.

Fig. 6.4 Web Page Containing Information for our Blog

Next, click the **Tools** menu option and select **Blog This in Windows Live Writer** from the drop-down menu.

This opens Windows Live Writer with the link to the Web page already inserted into it. Below, we have typed a few lines in the text area to indicate what the blog is about.

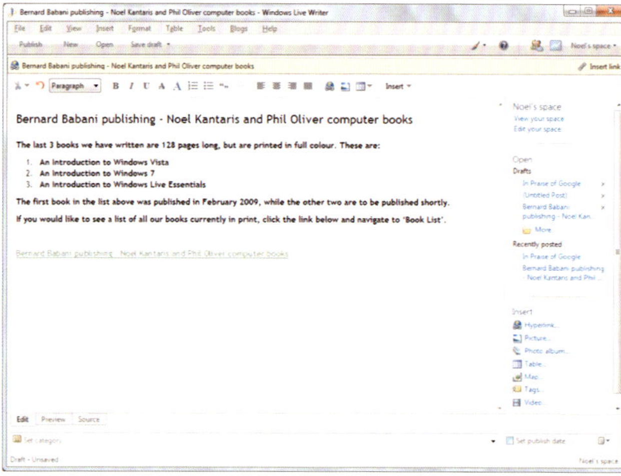

Fig. 6.5 Web Page Containing Information for our Blog

At this stage it might be a good idea to save your work by clicking the **Save Draft** button Save draft, followed by clicking the **Edit your space** link to be found on the right of the screen. This opens the screen below in an Internet Explorer window.

Fig. 6.6 The Edit My Space Screen

From here you can control who has access to your blog by clicking the **People I select** link and choosing either **Everyone (public)**, people in your **Network**, or specify individuals from your **Contacts List**. When you finish, press the **Save** button to save your settings. Once this is done, you have access to the **View your space** link. In the displayed screen you can also edit your profile, including what you want to be displayed about yourself.

Returning to the Windows Live Writer screen you can now select the date to publish. Clicking the **Publish** button Publish uploads your blog to the Web and opens automatically an Internet Explorer window in which your blog is displayed.

Creating a Blog from Scratch

To create a blog from scratch, start Windows Live Writer, or if it is already open click the **New** button, to open the screen below.

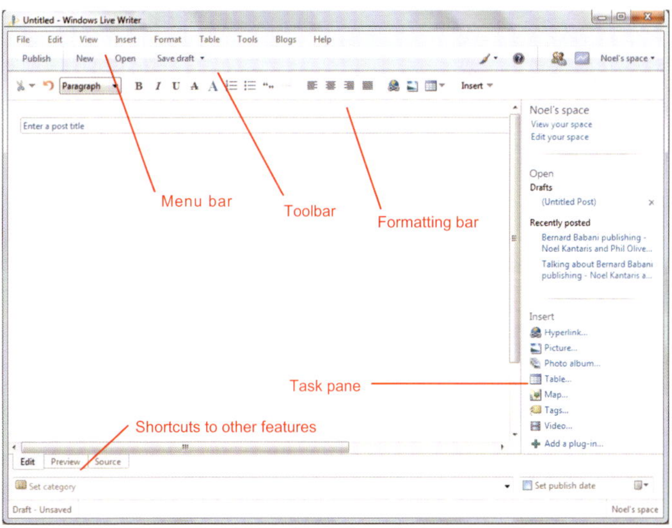

Fig. 6.7 The New Blog Screen

Note the **Formatting** toolbar at the top and the list of items in the Task pane on the right that you can use to **Insert** photos, videos, hyperlinks, etc., in your blog.

The Menu Bar Options

Each menu option has associated with it a pull-down sub-menu. Left-clicking a Menu bar option, reveals the pull-down sub-menu associated with it. Fig. 6.8 shows the sub-menu commands of the **File** option which are largely self-explanatory.

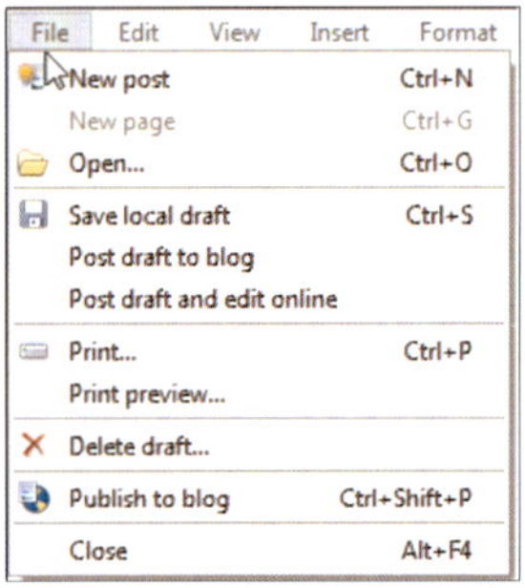

Fig. 6.8 The File Sub-menu

Some of the sub-menu commands can be accessed with 'quick key' combinations from the keyboard. These are shown on the drop-down menus. For example, **Ctrl+S** is the quick key for the **Save local draft** option in the **File** sub-menu. If a sub-menu option is not available at any time, like New page above, it will display in a grey colour.

Shortcut Menus

A context-sensitive shortcut menu is also available for the text entry area of Live Writer. If you click the right mouse button on any part of this area of the screen, a shortcut menu is displayed with the most frequently used commands, as shown here in Fig. 6.9, relating to text entry.

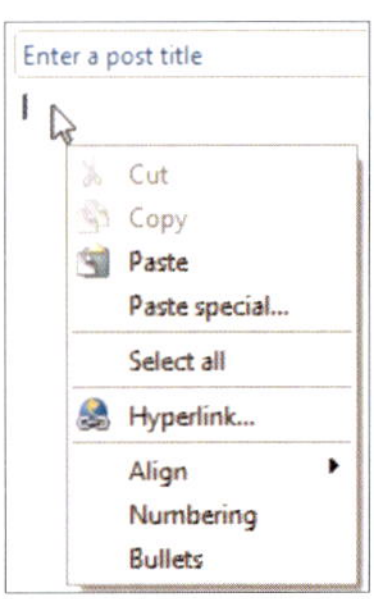

Fig. 6.9 A Shortcut Menu

Note that the **Cut** and **Copy** commands only become effective if you have some text selected. Left-clicking one of the options in the shortcut menu selects that option, while clicking on an area outside the shortcut menu (or pressing the **Esc** key), closes down the shortcut menu.

Note that some options in a shortcut menu can also be found in the **Edit** sub-menu, while others can be found in the sub-menu of the **Insert** option on the **Formatting** toolbar or the Task pane. Use whichever is more convenient for you.

Entering Text

To illustrate some of Live Writer's capabilities, you need to have a short text at hand. You might like to type the text below, but to see what is shown here, maximise Live Writer's window (click the button on its window), and start a new paragraph (by pressing **Enter**) after a colon (**:**) or semicolon (**;**) as shown in Fig. 6.10 below. Don't worry if the length of the lines in our example differs from those on your display.

It might not be generally known that Google is more than a Web Search engine. In fact, you can use:

Google Product Search and Google Checkout to make your online shopping quick and easy;

Google News to keep up-to-date with news;

Google Finance to get an instant up-to-date and historical data on stocks and shares, mutual funds and companies;

Gmail to send and receive emails;

Google Docs to create organise and share your documents, spreadsheets and presentations;

Picasa to organise and share your photos;

YouTube to search for view and upload your videos on to the Internet;

Google Maps to view maps and find local business information, how to get driving directions and traffic information, view satellite imagery and walk through street views of many places of the World;

Google Earth to 'fly' anywhere on Earth and view satellite imagery, maps terrain, street views and 3D buildings.

Fig. 6.10 The Beginnings of a Blog

As you type in text, any time you want to force a new line, or paragraph, just press the **Enter** key – Live Writer does not support word wrap. If you make a mistake while typing, press the **backspace** (**BkSp**) key enough times to erase it and start again. Finally, you can move the cursor around a document with the normal direction keys listed below.

To move	***Press***
Left one character	⇦
Right one character	⇨
Up one line	⇧
Down one line	⇩

Editing and Formatting Text

For small deletions, such as letters or words, the easiest method is to use the **Delete** (**Del**) or **Backspace** (**BkSp**) keys. To remove a character with the **Del** key, position the cursor to the left of the first character you want to remove and press **Del**; the character is deleted and the following text moves one space to the left. With the **BkSp** key, position the cursor to the right of the character you want to delete and press **BkSp**; the cursor moves one space to the left pulling the rest of the line with it, overwriting the character to be deleted.

When larger scale editing is needed you have several alternatives. You could first 'select' the text to be altered (see below), then use the **Cut, Copy** and **Paste** buttons, shown here, and available in the **Edit** sub-menu. Alternatively, you could use the quick key combinations, **Ctrl+X** to cut, **Ctrl+C** to copy, and **Ctrl+V** to paste. These operations are carried out via the system Clipboard.

To select text with the keyboard, position the insertion pointer on the first character to be selected and hold down the **Shift** key while using the arrow keys to highlight the required text, then release the **Shift** key.

To select text with the mouse, press down the left mouse button at the beginning of the block and while holding it pressed, drag the cursor across the block so that the desired text is highlighted, then release the mouse button.

Once text has been selected it can be copied to another location in your present document, to another Live Writer document, or indeed to another Windows application.

To change our blog to what is shown on the next page, do the following:

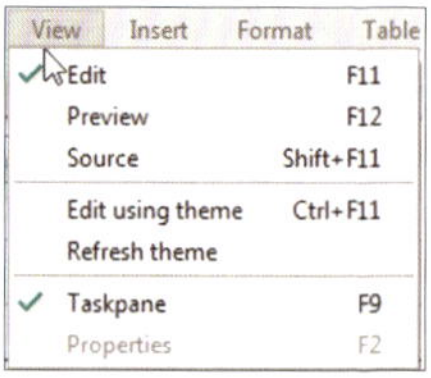

Fig. 6.11 The View Menu Options

- Click the **View** menu command and make sure that the option **Edit using theme** is not ticked. If it is click on it to remove it.

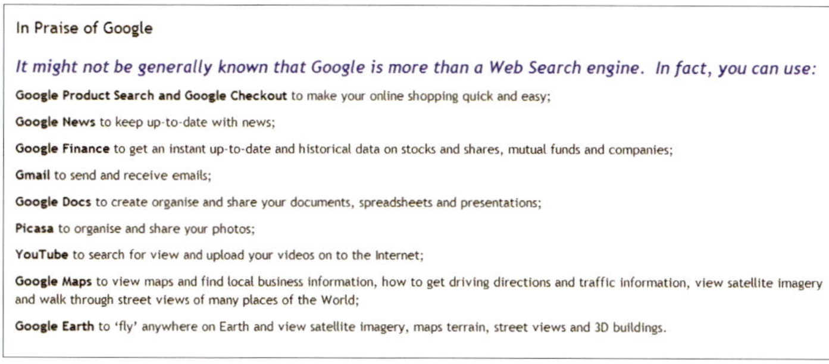
In Praise of Google

It might not be generally known that Google is more than a Web Search engine. In fact, you can use:

Google Product Search and Google Checkout to make your online shopping quick and easy;

Google News to keep up-to-date with news;

Google Finance to get an instant up-to-date and historical data on stocks and shares, mutual funds and companies;

Gmail to send and receive emails;

Google Docs to create organise and share your documents, spreadsheets and presentations;

Picasa to organise and share your photos;

YouTube to search for view and upload your videos on to the Internet;

Google Maps to view maps and find local business information, how to get driving directions and traffic information, view satellite imagery and walk through street views of many places of the World;

Google Earth to 'fly' anywhere on Earth and view satellite imagery, maps terrain, street views and 3D buildings.

Fig. 6.12 The Edited Blog Text

To make the rest of the changes shown above in Fig. 6.12, do the following:

- Click the **Enter post Title** area and type the words **In Praise of Google**.
- In the main text area, select the first line, then click the **Font** icon on the **Formatting** bar A, to display the Font box shown in Fig. 6.13 below.

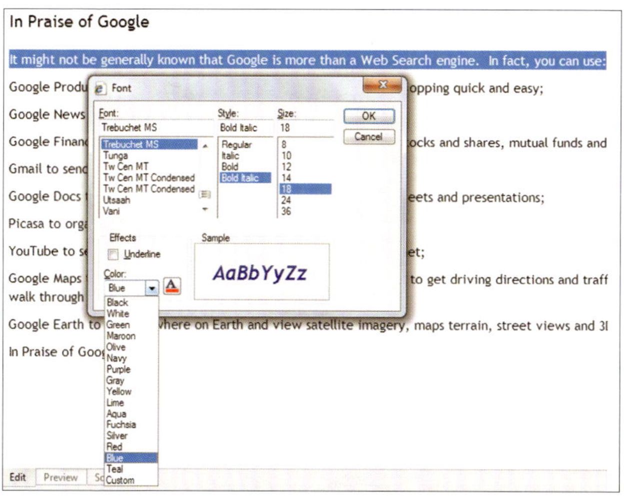

Fig. 6.13 The Font Dialogue Box

- Click the down-arrow under **Color** to open the drop-down list of colours and select **Blue**. Next, click the

Bold Italic option. In this dialogue box you can change the **Font** type and its size. Click **OK** to action the changes made so far.

- Place the insertion pointer anywhere in the newly changed first line of the main text and click the down-arrow against the **Change Text Style** button and select **Heading 1** from the drop-down list. The changes take effect immediately, increasing the font size of the text.
- Select, in turn, each title of Google's applications listed in the main text area and click the **Bold** icon on the **Formatting** bar, as shown in Fig. 6.14 for the first two titles.

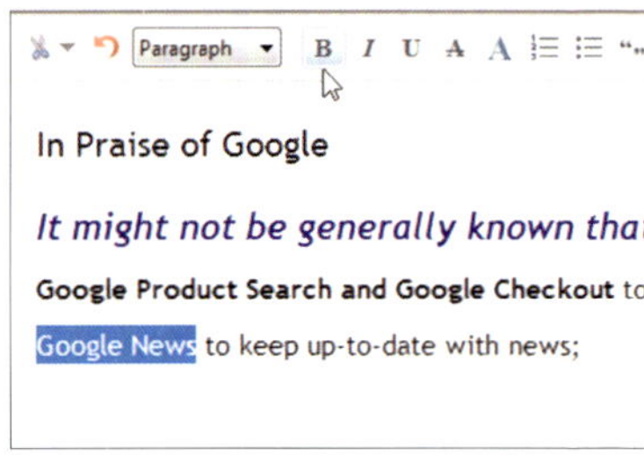

Fig. 6.14 Emboldening Titles

Every so often while editing your blog, click the  icon at the top of the Live Writer window to save your work. To preview it, click the **Preview** 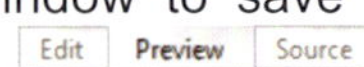 button at the bottom of Live Writer window, while to continue with your editing, click the **Edit** button.

When you are satisfied with your changes to your blog, click the  button on the toolbar to publish your work, which will be displayed in your browser as follows.

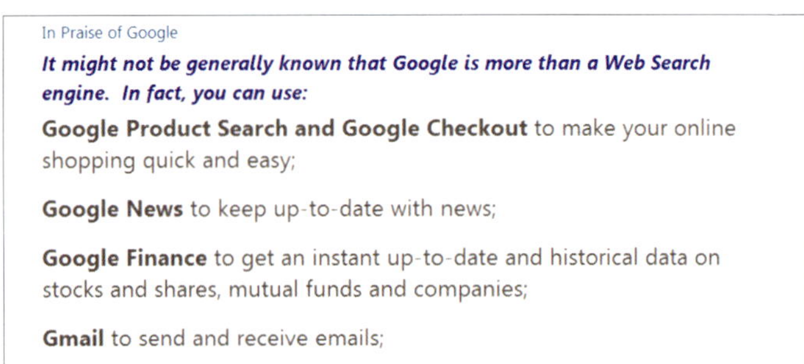

Fig. 6.15 Part of our Published Blog

Inserting Pictures in a Blog

To insert a picture in your blog, click the **Picture** link under the **Insert** entry in the Task pane, shown here in Fig. 6.16. Next, navigate to where the picture you want to insert is to be found, and click it. For us, the result is as shown in Fig. 6.17.

Fig. 6.16

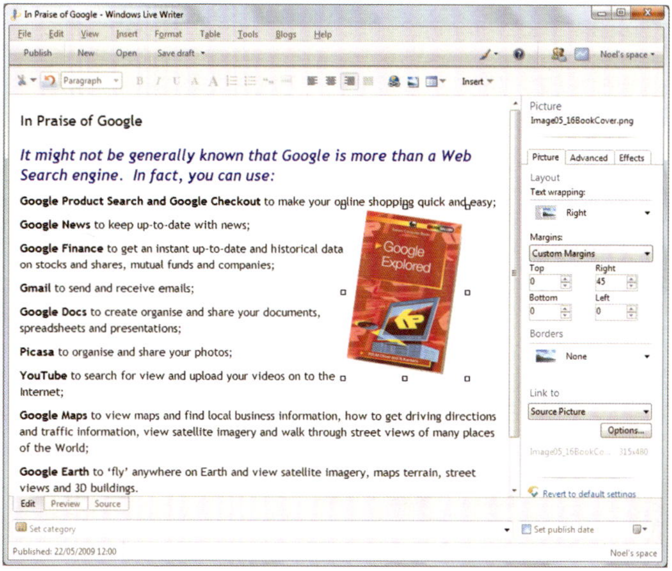

Fig. 6.17 Inserting a Picture in a Blog

The contents of the Task pane are now replaced by a 3-tab options screen, provided the picture is selected. Above we show the contents of the Picture tab in which you can select the **Layout** of the picture from a drop-down list – you can choose between Inline, Left, Right, and Center. Unfortunately there is no option to wrap text around a picture.

The distance of the picture from the right edge of the screen is controlled by the Right margin option, while the size of the picture can be made smaller by placing the mouse pointer on one of the corner handles and when it changes to an inclined two headed arrow ↘, move it towards the centre of the picture. To increase the size of the picture, drag the inclined two headed arrow pointer away from the picture.

To move the picture vertically within the text area, place the mouse pointer on the picture and when it is changed into a four-headed arrow ✥, drag the picture up or down.

The tilting of the picture is controlled from the Advanced tab, shown here in Fig. 6.18, together with those of the Effects tab.

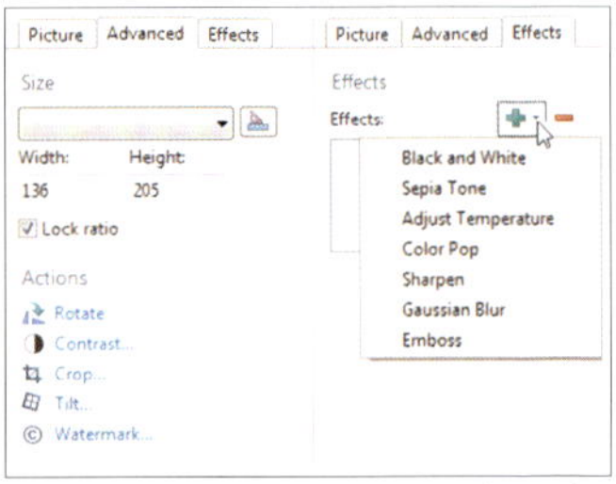

Fig. 6.18 The Advanced and Effects Tab Screen Options

Live Writer allows you to select a group of pictures and place them within your blog. To do so, click the **Photo Album** link under the **Insert** entry in the Task pane (see Fig. 6.16). This opens the dialogue box shown on the right of Fig. 6.19 into which you drag a selection of photos, as shown.

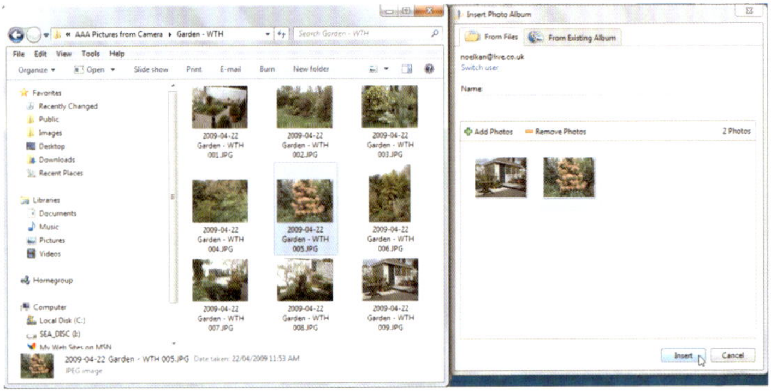

Fig. 6.19 Dragging Pictures into the Insert Album Box

Use Windows Explorer to navigate to where the photos you want to include in your blog are to be found. Arrange the two windows side-by-side, as shown above, then if you want to select all the photos in a folder, use the **Ctrl+A** key combination to highlight them all and drag them with the left mouse button depressed into the Insert Album Box. Alternatively, you can drag each photo in turn.

Finally, give the album a name, and click the **Insert** button to place the album in your blog.

In Fig. 6.20 below, we chose the selected photos in a **Scatter Album style**.

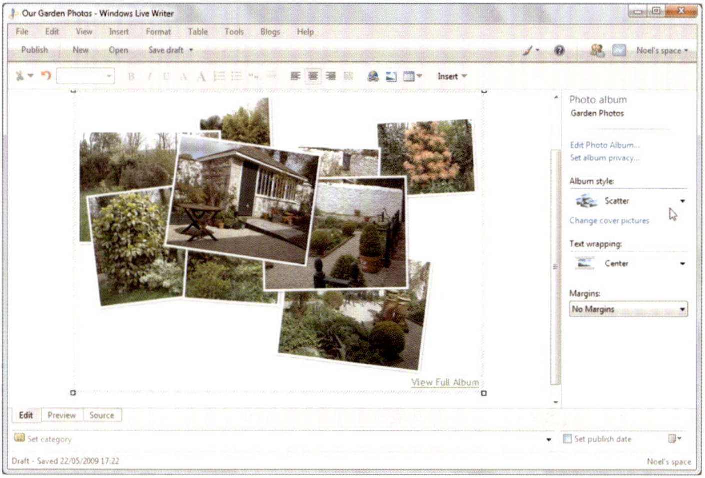

Fig. 6.20 Inserting an Album in a Blog in a Scatter Style

To see all the **Album style** options available to you, click the down-arrow pointed to in Fig. 6.21 to the left.

Fig. 6.21 Available Album

Inserting a Table in a Blog

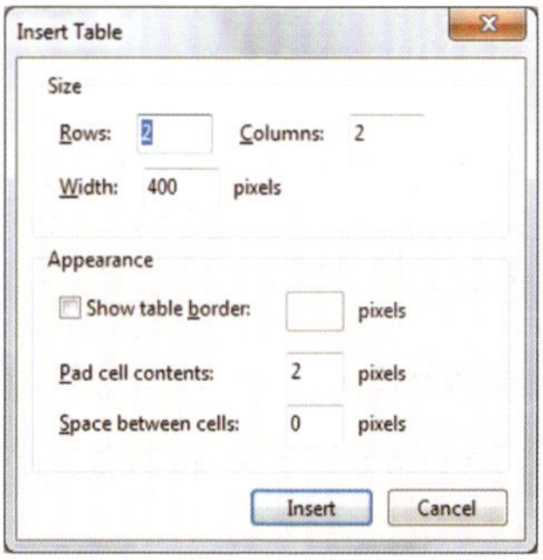

You can insert a table in your blog by clicking the **Table** link under the **Insert** entry in the Task pane (see Fig. 6.16). This opens the dialogue box shown in Fig. 6.22, in which you can specify the number of rows and columns you require.

Fig. 6.22 The Insert Table Box

Inserting a Video in a Blog

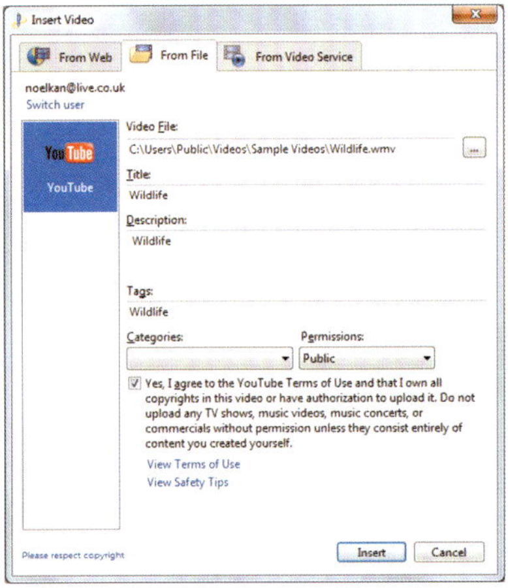

Fig. 6.23 The Insert Video Box

Live Writer makes it extremely easy to add a video to your blog. Click the **Video** link under the **Insert** entry in the Task pane (see Fig. 6.16), to open the window shown in Fig. 6.23.

Here, we clicked the From File tab which caused Live Writer to search for all the files on our PC containing videos. We chose the one called 'wildlife.wmv'.

Live Writer provides you with the YouTube site to store your video. The site requires you to sign up and agree to their terms and conditions, before you can proceed. It is as simple as that!

Editing or Deleting Individual Postings

Sometimes you might want to edit or delete individual postings which are already in your Blog Space. How to do this is not immediately obvious, so we will take you through the necessary steps.

In a **New** Live Writer window, click the **Edit your space** link to be found at the top of the Task pane, as shown here in Fig. 6.24.

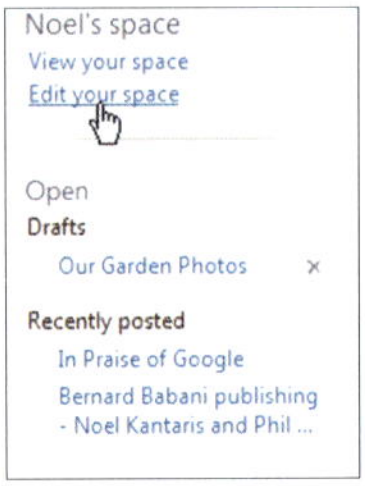

When the **Edit space** screen opens, left-click the title of the posting you want to edit or delete, as shown in Fig. 6.25 on the next page.

Fig. 6.24 Available Album

Fig. 6.25 Left-clicking a Postings Title you want to Edit or Delete

This opens another screen with the **Edit** and **Delete** buttons in it, as shown in Fig. 6.26 below.

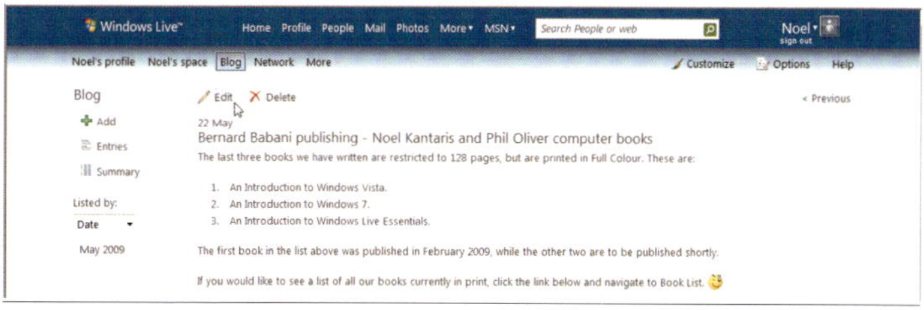

Fig. 6.26 The Screen from which you can Edit or Delete a Posting

To delete the posting from your Blog Space, click the **Delete** button. To edit the posting, click the **Edit** button to display the screen in Fig. 6.27.

Fig. 6.27 The Edit a Posting Screen

As you can see, the editing facilities here have additional formatting functionality, such as being able to increase or decrease text indent, insert a search link, insert a line, use text highlight colouring, and add emoticons (short for emotion icons). Having edited your posting, don't forget to **Publish** it again.

Deleting a Blog Space

To delete your entire Blog Space with all its postings (so you can start afresh), click the **Edit your space** link at the top of the Task pane, and on the next screen click **Options** and select **General**, as shown here in Fig. 6.28.

Fig. 6.28 Available Album

This opens yet another screen at the very bottom of which you will see the **Delete your space** button with a warning above it, as shown in Fig. 6.29.

Fig. 6.29 The Screen from which you can Delete your Space

Getting Help with Live Writer

To open the Live Writer's Help screen, click the Help icon on the Toolbar.

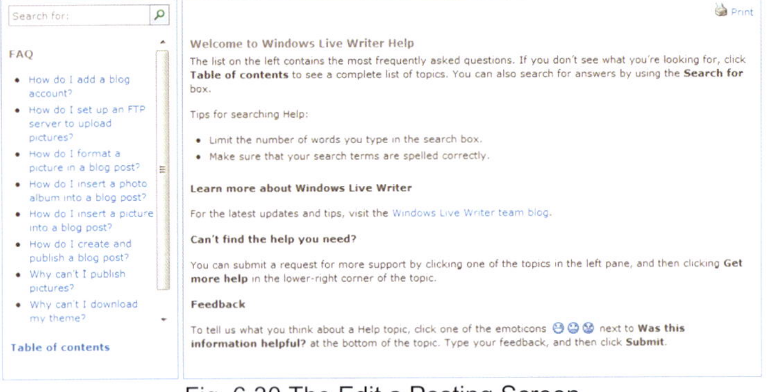

Fig. 6.30 The Edit a Posting Screen

It is worth spending some time here as there is a lot more to Live Writer than we were able to cover in the available space. We hope we have given you sufficient basic information, to have the confidence to try the rest for yourself. Have fun!

7

Windows Live Movie Maker

With **Windows Live Movie Maker** you can edit and rearrange your home-made video cam movies, make a shorter version of them, add still pictures and voice-over, and either post them to the Web for all to see, or send them to your friends as an attachment to an e-mail.

The Live Movie Maker can be found in the **All Programs** listing. Clicking its icon starts the program and displays a screen similar to that shown in Fig. 7.1.

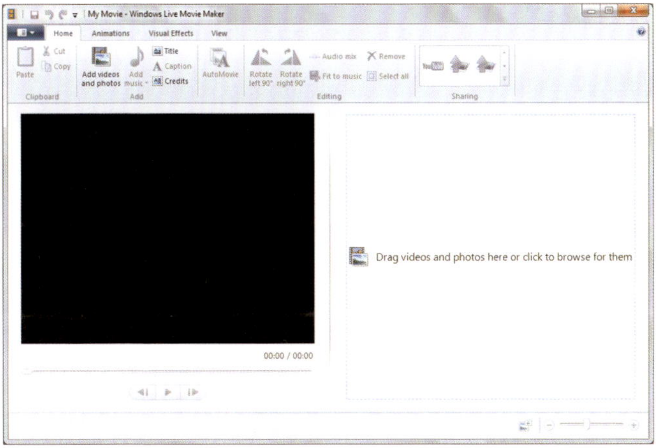

Fig. 7.1 The Windows Movie Maker Screen

The displayed screen is divided into three areas, with the top area showing the Ribbon which includes all of the available tasks you can apply to a project. Below the Ribbon there are two areas with the one to the right being where you drag your videos and photos, and the one to the left being the area where your project is played.

The Ribbon

Traditional menus and toolbars have been replaced in Live Movie Maker with the Ribbon – a device that presents commands organised into a set of tabs. Those of you who are familiar with Microsoft Office 2007 will be used to the Ribbon and know how to use it. But for those who are not familiar with this concept, we include here a short explanation of its functionality.

The tabs on the Ribbon display the commands that are most relevant for each of the task areas in the application, as shown in Fig. 7.2.

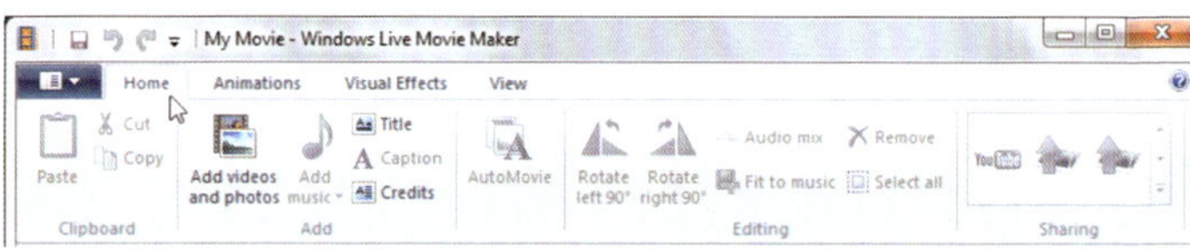

Fig. 7.2 The Home Tab of the Ribbon

There are four basic components to the Ribbon:

Tabs There are four basic tabs across the top, each representing an activity area – Home, Animations, Visual Effects, and View. Once a video is opened, an extra Edit tab appears.

Groups Each tab has several groups that show related items together, such as Clipboard, Add Editing, and Sharing for the Home tab.

Commands A command is a button, a box to enter information, or a menu. For example, for the Home tab and above the Add group there are commands such as Add videos and photos.

Clicking a new tab opens a new series of groups, each with its relevant command buttons. This really works very well. In addition, Live Movie Maker has an extra button to the left of the Home tab, called **File**. Clicking its down-arrow, opens the drop-down menu shown in Fig. 7.3 on the next page.

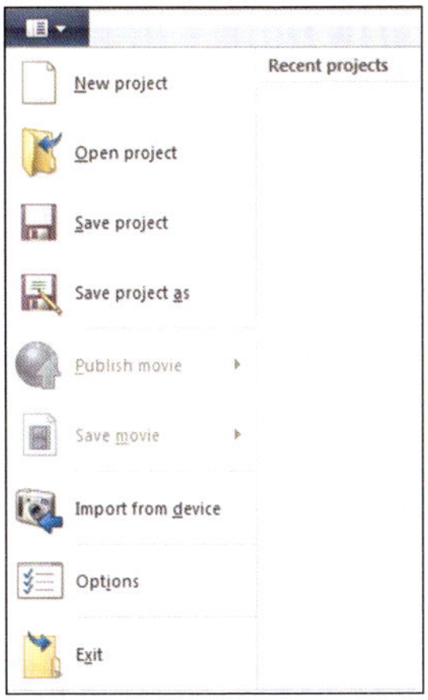

You use the **File** drop-down menu to create, open and save a project, as well as to set different options for Movie Maker (see Fig. 7.3).

However, here we will start a project by clicking the **Add Videos and photos** button on the Home tab of the Ribbon. This displays the collection of videos that Windows automatically placed in the **Sample Videos** Library folder during installation, as shown in Fig. 7.4.

Fig. 7.3 The File Drop-Down Menu

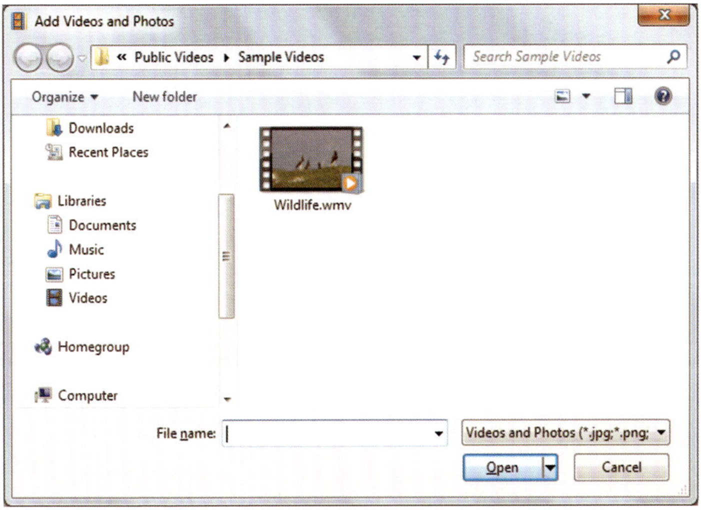

Fig. 7.4 The Windows Movie Maker Video Folder

The clip shown above came as a video sample with Windows 7. Note that apart from the **Videos** Library folder, you also have the **Pictures** and **Music** folders, the contents of which can be used for perhaps assembling a slide show with added music, fading effects, etc., which we will examine later.

Old Project Files into Video Files

By now you may have discovered that attempting to open in Live Movie Maker files with the extension **.mswmm** made with the previous version of Windows Movie Maker, results in the display of a warning box similar to the one shown in Fig. 7.5 below.

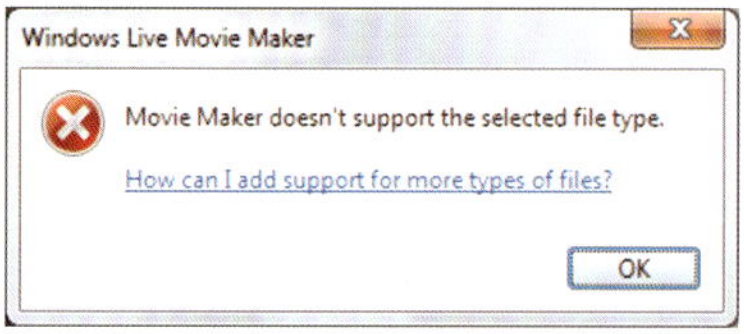

Fig. 7.5 The Warning Box

If you look at the properties of such a file, you might be able to assign a different program to open it, as shown in Fig. 7.6, but none of the applications offered will open it.

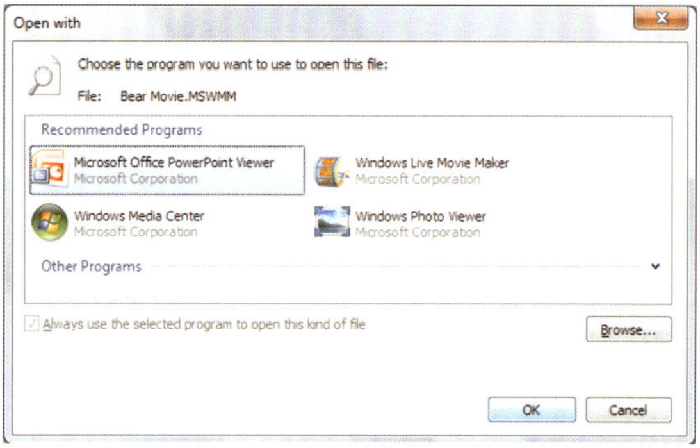

Fig. 7.6 Applications you Could Assign to Open the File

The reason for this is that the **.mswmm** files are actually **Project** files created with a previous version of Movie Maker; they only hold information on which clips to play at what time interval and for how long. In Fig. 7.5. Windows Live Movie Maker can not open such a file. The same thing will happen if you select a different application for opening such a file. To be able to use such a file in Live Movie Maker, you must first convert it to a **.wmv** (video) file.

To do this, open it in the Windows Vista version of Movie Maker that was used to create it, as shown in Fig. 7.7.

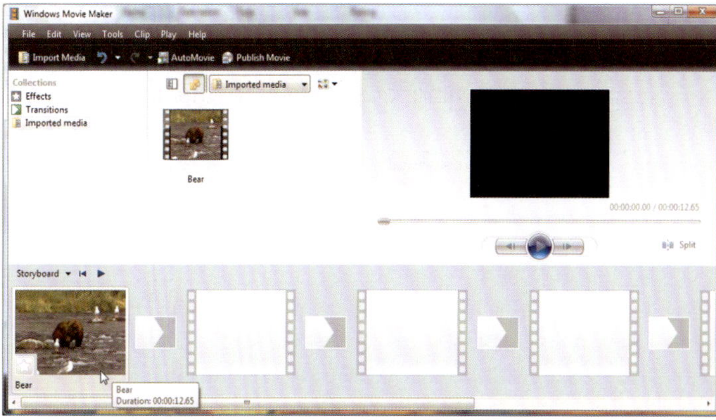

Fig. 7.7 A Project File Opened in the Windows Movie Maker it was Created in

Above, we also show the Project file dragged onto the **Storyboard**. Doing so, activates the **Publish Movie** button on the Movie Maker's toolbar and makes it usable. Clicking the **Publish Movie** button displays the screen in Fig. 7.8.

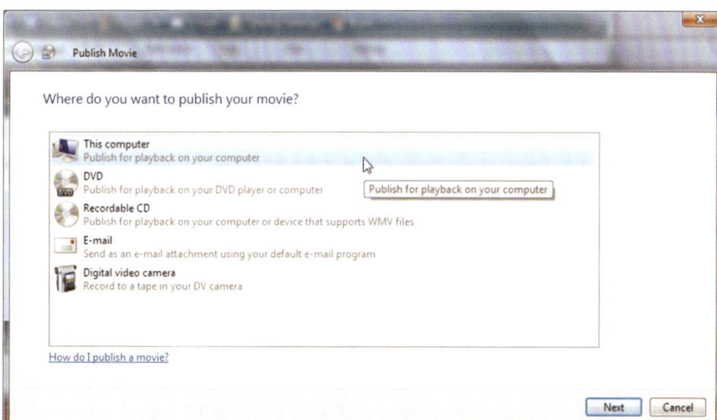

Fig. 7.8 The Publish Movie Dialogue Box

Next, select the option **This computer**, and click **Next** to open the next dialogue box, as shown in Fig. 7.9 overleaf.

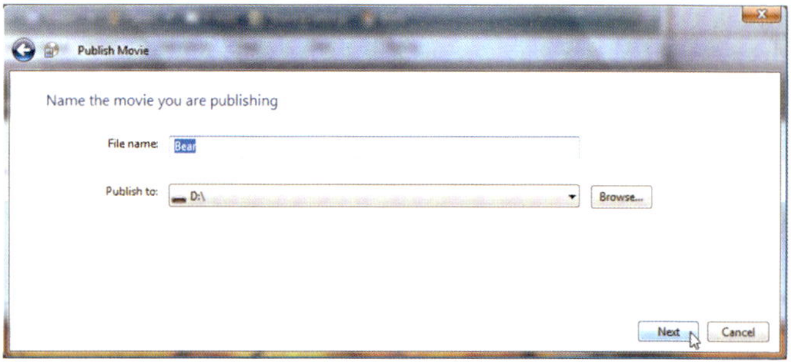

Fig. 7.9 Naming the Movie to be Published

Here we named the movie **Bear** and we published it to the D: drive, which is actually a memory stick attached to the Windows Vista computer, because we want to be able to transfer it to the PC running Windows 7 – make sure there is enough free space on the memory stick you are using. In this case the file was only 6.78 MB, but in your case it might be much larger. Clicking **Next**, opens the screen shown in Fig. 7.10.

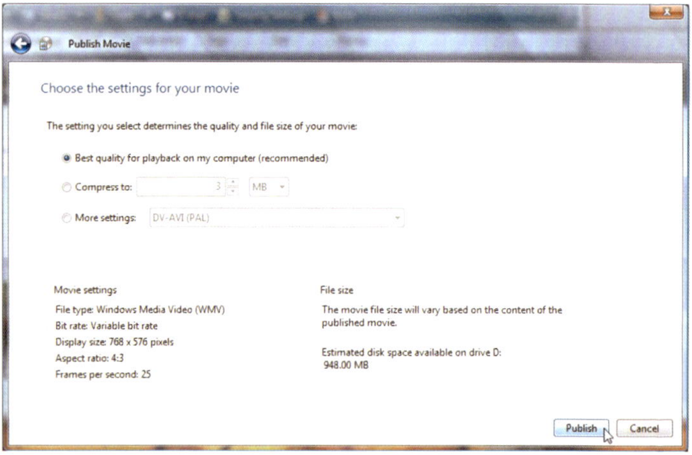

Fig. 7.10 Choosing the Settings for the Movie to be Published

Here we selected the option **Best quality for playback on my computer** and clicked the **Publish** button.

Playing a Converted Project File

Below, we show the file of the transferred movie which is now on the memory stick attached to our Windows 7 computer.

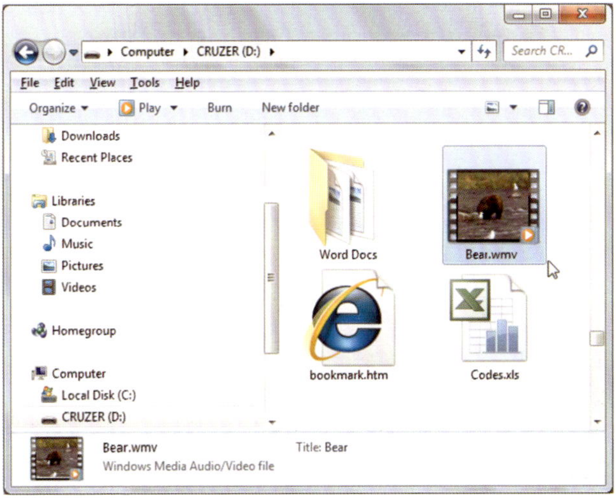

Fig. 7.11 The Transferred File and its Properties

As you can see above the file has a **.wmv** extension, but it is assigned to Windows Media Player. You can change this by clicking the **Change** button on the Properties dialogue box and selecting instead Windows Live Movie Maker from the available choices. Double-clicking the file, opens it in the selected application, as shown in Fig. 7.12 below.

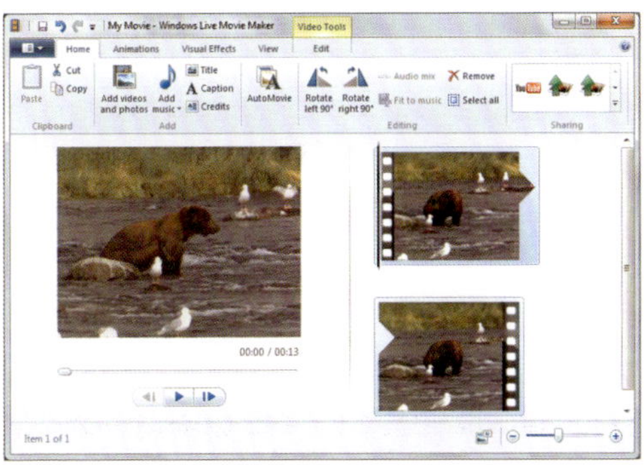

Fig. 7.12 The Transferred File Loaded in Windows Live Movie

Video Editing

We will use the **Wildlife** video as an example to show the editing abilities of Movie Maker. To begin the process, start Movie Maker and click the **Add videos and photos** button shown selected in the composite of Fig. 7.13. This opens the **Sample Video** folder showing for us the two available videos. Double-clicking the **Wildlife** file opens it in Movie Maker, as shown in Fig. 7.14 on the next page.

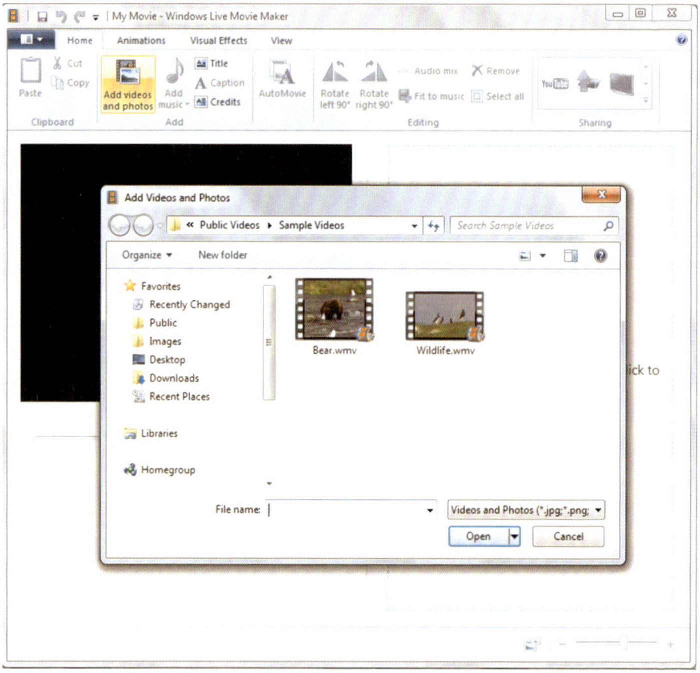

Fig. 7.13 Selecting a Video to Insert in the Movie Maker Screen

On the top of the Movie Maker screen there is the usual Ribbon containing the Tabs, Groups and Commands available to you at that time. These Tabs, Groups and Commands change once a video file is inserted in the **Workspace** area, as seen in Fig. 7.14, where we have also selected the Edit tab on the Ribbon.

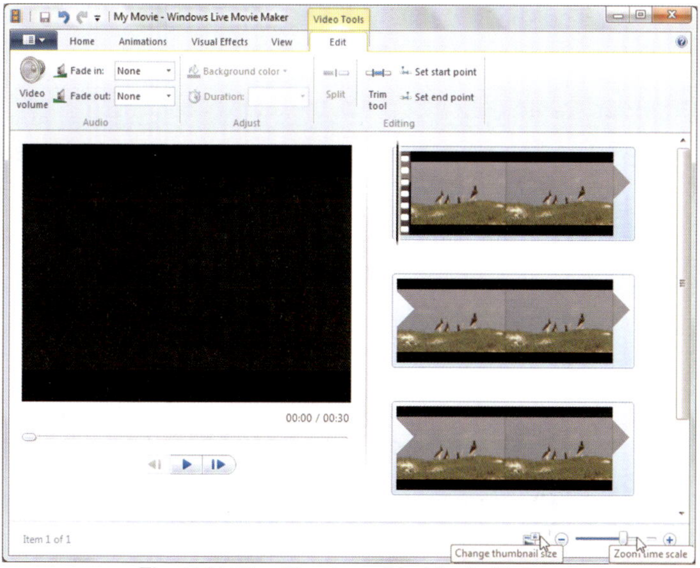

Fig. 7.14 The Storyboard in Movie Maker

It is here that you assemble or edit your movie – with the **Storyboard** focusing on sequencing. Also note the two useful tools at the bottom of the screen; the **Zoom time scale**, and the **Change thumbnail size**.

As you drag the **Zoom time scale** handle to the right the **Storyboard** expands, which allows you to locate desired points in a video more accurately. Clicking the **Change thumbnail size** icon, displays a menu which gives you the option to change the size of the displayed thumbnails. Do try these to see how they work.

Finally have a close look at the available editing tools in the Edit tab which include the **Split** tool and the **Trim** tool, both of which can be used in editing a video. Other tools on the Ribbon allow you to synchronise video clips with audio clips, or create fading transitions between clips.

You can start the **Wildlife** video by clicking the **Play** button below the **Preview** pane, or by pressing the **Space** bar on the keyboard. To stop a video click the **Pause** button, or press the **Space** bar on the keyboard once more.

You can also move through a video frame by frame. To go forward, click the **Next frame** button or press the **L** keyboard key (see Fig. 7.15 below), while to go backwards, click the **Previous frame** button or press the **J** keyboard key.

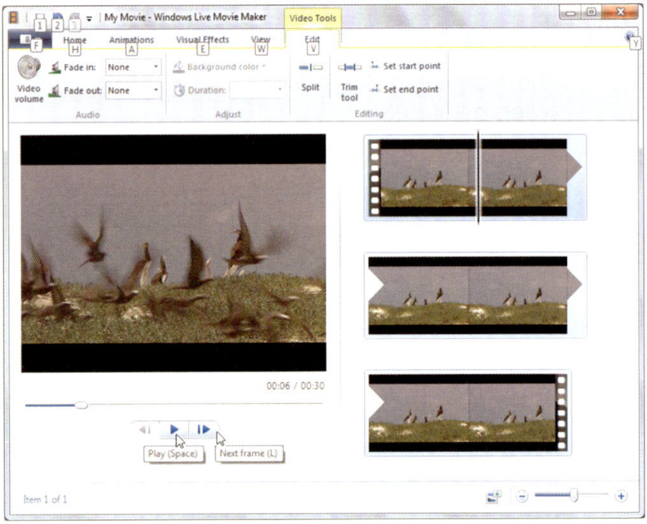

Fig. 7.15 Playing a Video

If you continue watching the video you will come across several frames in which alarmed birds take off and their wings obscure the birds on the hill, as shown above. We are only using this as an example of how to remove such offending frames from a video. After all, it could be a waving hand that momentarily obscured a bride's face in a wedding video and spoils the whole precious moment!

To remove unwanted frames, stop the video at the first offending place and use the **Previous Frame** and **Next Frame** controls to move it a fraction of a second before the offending instance, then click the **Split** button on the Edit tab. Next, find the last offending frame and split the video again. Finally, remove the offending frames by right-clicking them and selecting **Remove** from the drop-down menu. To save your creation, use the **File**, **Save Project As** menu command. To recover your edited project later, use the **File**, **Open** command.

Creating a Slide Movie

You can use Movie Maker to create a slide show. As an example we will use some of the pictures in the **Sample Pictures** folder to be found in the **Public** folder that came with Windows 7. To do so, click the **Add videos and photos** button on the Home tab and navigate to **Pictures**, **Sample Pictures** folder, pointed to in Fig. 7.16 below.

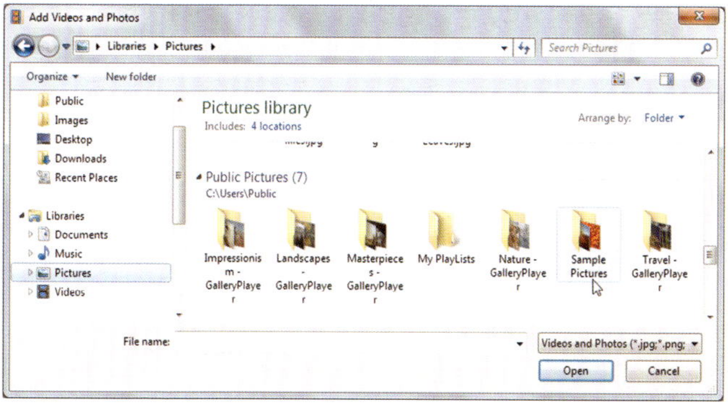

Fig. 7.16 Selecting Pictures for a Slide Show

Clicking this folder, opens it to reveal its contents. We selected five pictures with a common theme – flowers. You could, of course use your own selection of pictures.

Fig. 7.17 The Selected Pictures for the Slide Show

To rearrange the sequence of these pictures, drag them in the **Workspace** area and place them in the sequence you want them to appear in your slide show.

You can import an audio file that plays while the slide show is actually displaying. To do so, go to the start of the first slide, click the **Select all** command in the **Editing** group on the Home tab, then use the **Add music** button on the Home tab and select **Add music at the current point**. This opens your **Music** folder from which either choose your own (short) music, or open the **Sample Music** folder and select one from the displayed list, as shown in Fig. 7.18.

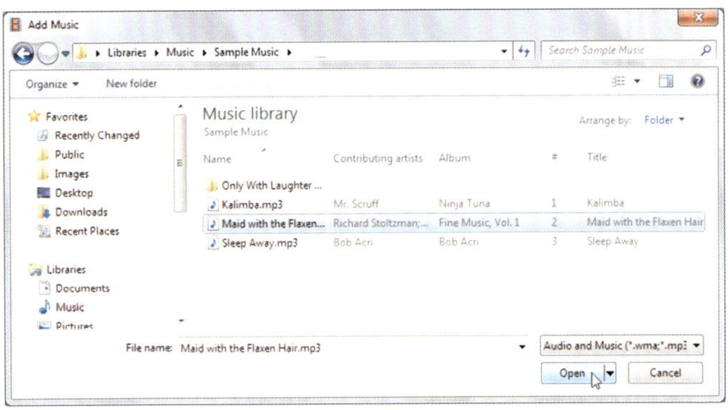

Fig. 7.18 Selecting a Music Track for the Slide Show

Selecting a short track (the one above is less than 3 minutes long), and clicking **Open**, includes your music selection with the chosen pictures and returns you to Movie Maker.

You can also include 'transitions' between pictures so that you do not have abrupt changes from one picture to the other. To do this, select all the pictures again, then click the Animations tab and select the **Crossfade** transition, pointed to in Fig. 7.19 below.

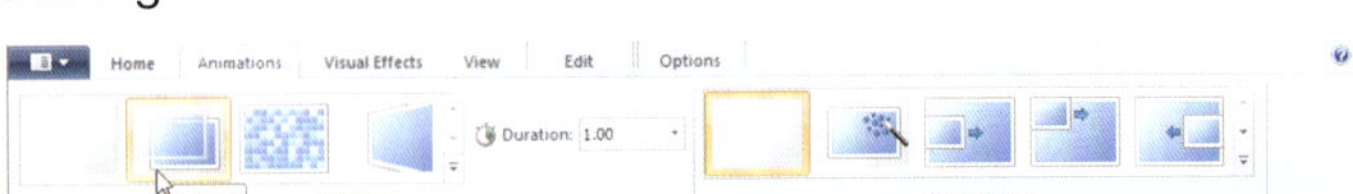

Fig. 7.19 The Visual Effects Tab Options

As you can see, there are also visual effects you could apply to your creation, but we leave that to you to experiment with.

Next, click the Edit tab on the Ribbon and note the default transition time of 5.00 seconds pointed to in Fig. 7.20 below which can be changed to suit your needs, by clicking the down-arrow and selecting from the drop-down list.

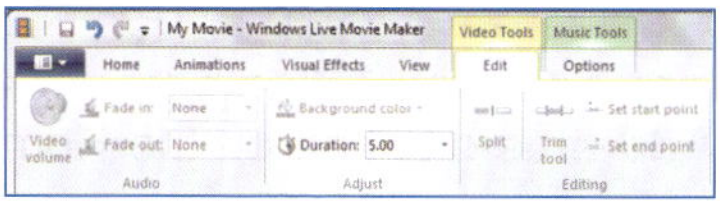

Fig. 7.20 The Edit Tab Options

Fig. 7.21 The Home Tab Options

There is, however, another way of setting the duration of the time interval, particularly if you have chosen to include music in your slide show. To do this, click the Home tab on the Ribbon and select the **Fit to music** option pointed to in Fig. 7.21.

What this does is to adjust the transition time of your slide show to fit the actual length of the selected music. This is why we chose a rather short music track.

Test your creation by clicking the **Play** button. Note the position of the Playing monitor at the bottom left of the screen, pointed to in Fig. 7.22.

Fig. 7.22 Playing the Newly Created Movie

The screen dump above was taken just as the second picture was about to appear in the preview area, 33 seconds from the start of the movie.

Finally, select all the adjusted picture frames, then click the **More** options button in the **Sharing** group, pointed to in Fig. 7.23(a) to open all the available options, as shown in Fig. 7.23(b).

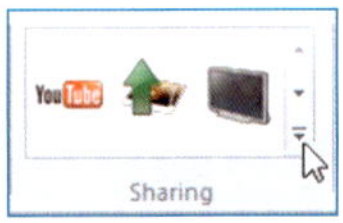

(a)

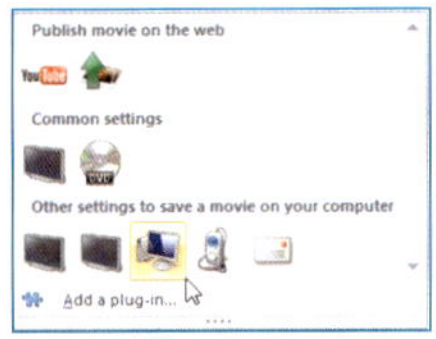

(b)

Fig. 7.23 Creating your Movie

For testing purposes, we suggest you select the option pointed to in Fig. 7.23(b) as it will take less time to create the movie. When you are satisfied with your efforts you could select to burn your creation on a DVD or publish it on the Web. The created movie will be saved by default in your user's **Videos** folder under the name **My Movie**, unless you change it. After it is created, a dialogue box is displayed and clicking the **Play** button, starts playing the movie.

Having gone through the above, now start a new project, drag the same pictures into the working area, then click on the **AutoMovie** button and follow the instructions and save the result as a project. Do try it!

Publishing to a Social Network

To publish photos or a video, click the **Home** tab, then click the **More** options button in the **Sharing** group, as discussed above, and select the **Add a plug-in** option from the drop-down menu, as shown in Fig. 7.24.

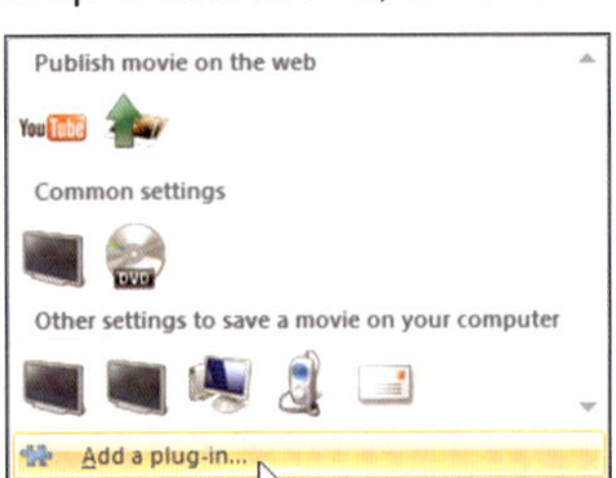

Fig. 7.24 Adding a Plug-in

From here we can download the Facebook plug-in, from the displayed Web site.

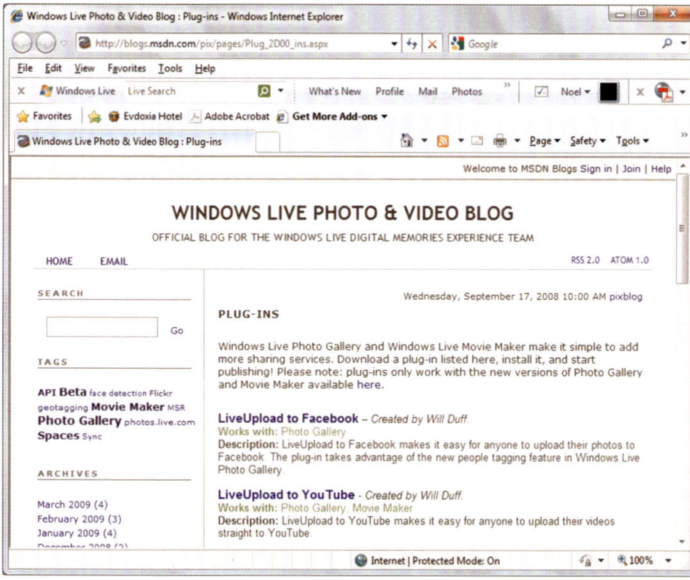

Fig. 7.25 The Plug-ins for Uploading Pictures and Videos

The **Live Upload to Facebook** plug-in, when downloaded and installed, appears as an additional option on the **Home**, **Sharing** group. It also appears on the **Publish**, **More Services** sub-menu of Live Photo Gallery.

The **Facebook** button, pointed to in Fig. 7.26, is used to upload only pictures to Facebook, while the **YouTube** button (see Fig. 7.27) is used to upload either pictures or videos to YouTube; these two being amongst the most popular social networking sites.

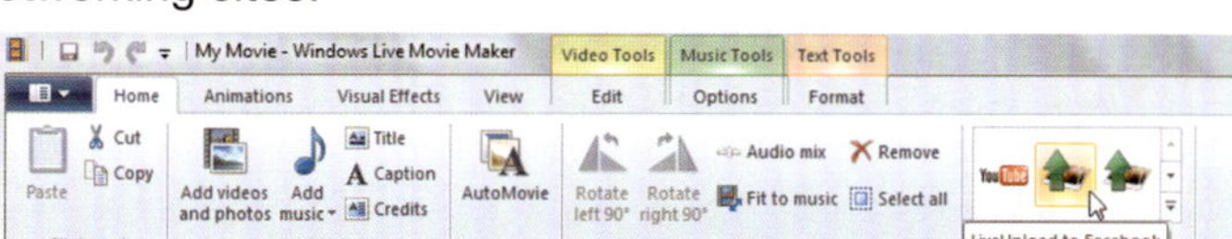

Fig. 7.26 The Visual Effects Tab Options

Also, do checkout the various options available in the Format tab shown above.

To upload your newly created video to one of the social networks, say YouTube, click the **Publish on YouTube** button shown here in Fig. 7.27. YouTube asks you to sign in into your YouTube account (if you don't have one you must first create it), and displays the screen shown in Fig. 7.28.

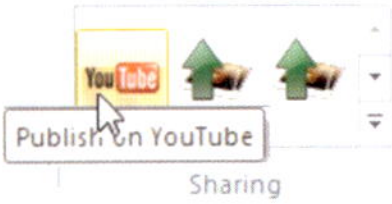

Fig. 7.27

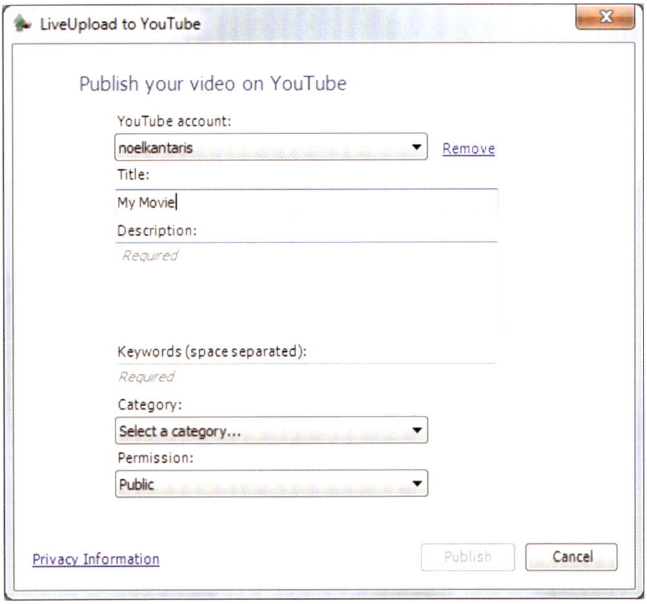

Fig. 7.28 Creating our Own Video Space on YouTube

After entering the required information, click the **Publish** button. Live Movie Maker first converts your movie to a format suitable for publication, then publishes it on YouTube.

It takes some time before you can see your uploaded video, then a bit more time before the video is released to the general public.

* * *

We leave it to you to explore additional Movie Maker capabilities. Have fun!

8

Windows Live Toolbar

The Windows Live Toolbar is inserted in Internet Explorer, as shown in Fig. 8.1 below, so that all the Live applications are available to you from there.

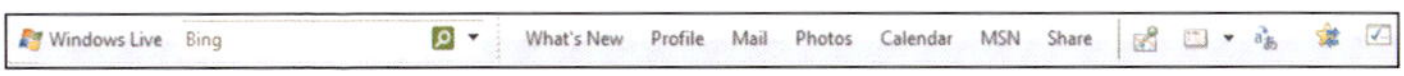

Fig. 8.1 The Windows Live Toolbar

Configuring IE for Live Toolbar

For the selection of options on the Live Toolbar to work correctly, you need to configure Internet Explorer, as follows:

- Start Internet Explorer, click the **Tools** menu option and select **Internet Options** from the sub-menu to open a dialogue box by the same name.
- In the Security tab of the displayed dialogue box, click the **Custom level** button at the bottom of the box.
- In the Security Settings box that opens, scroll down to **Active X controls and plug-ins** and click the **Enable** radio button, then scroll even further down to **Active scripting** and click the **Enable** radio button.
- In the Privacy tab, click the **Default** button and slide the displayed slider under **Settings**, to a security level of **Medium High** or lower.
- In the Advanced tab, in the **Security** section, select the **Warn if changing between secure and not secure mode** check box to turn off this option.

Finally, click **OK** and **Yes** on the displayed warning box, and **Apply** on the Internet Options dialogue box, followed by **OK**.

The Search Facility

Clicking the down-arrow to the right of the Search text box, reveals a drop-down menu, as shown here in Fig. 8.2, from which you can direct your search to specific areas. For example, typing **Moon** in the **Search** box, then pointing and clicking **Images**, opens the application **bing** and displays all the images of the moon it can find, as shown in Fig. 8.3.

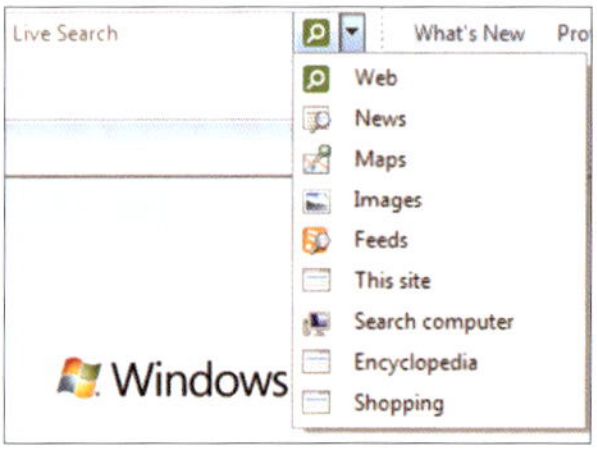

Fig. 8.2 Live Search Areas

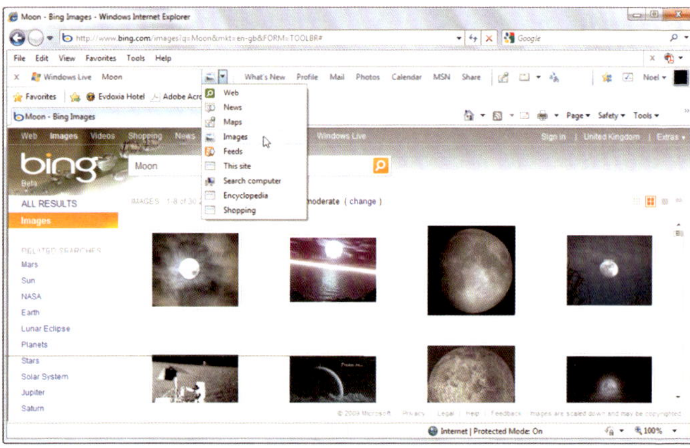

Fig. 8.3 The Result of an Image Search

What's New in your Network

Clicking the **What's New** button (or indeed any of the other buttons on the Live Toolbar for the first time), opens the screen shown in Fig. 8.4. Click the **Sign in** button to open the text area where you type your password.

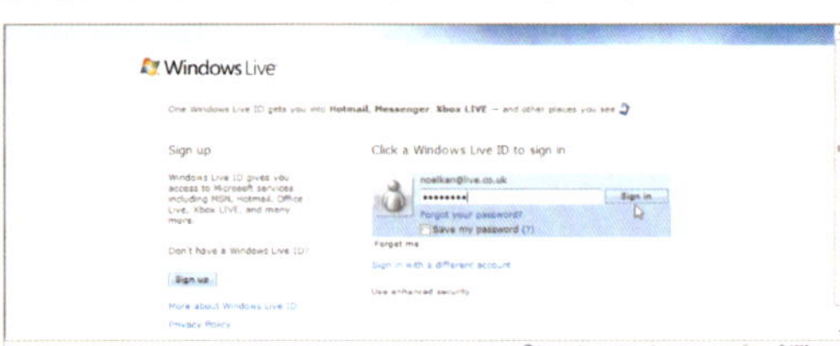

Fig. 8.4 Signing in to Windows Live

Clicking **Sign in** once more, opens a small screen, as shown at the top of Fig. 8.5. Clicking the **View more of what's new** link, loads and opens the actual screen of the selected Live Toolbar option. In Fig. 8.5 we show both screens open at the same time.

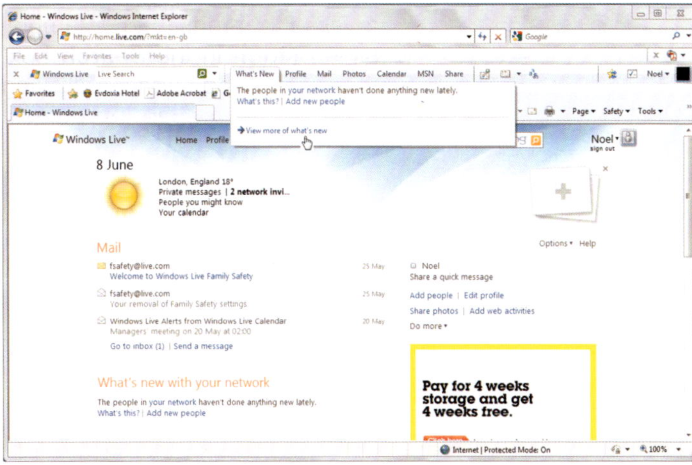

Fig. 8.5 What's New on your Network Screens

There is a wealth of options here which you can explore for yourself, including your latest e-mail messages, alerts from your Calendar, what's new that people in your network have done lately and posted their doings so you can look at them, and some inevitable advertisements! It seems that you can't get anything free these days without advertisements.

Your Profile Option

Clicking the **Profile** button, displays your profile and asks you to insert your occupation, location, and other details, if you haven't done so already, as shown in Fig. 8.6 on the next page.

As you can see, the application has also included our **Blog Images**, the ones we posted to our blog when discussing the subject earlier in the book. The displayed advertisement will most definitely be different for you.

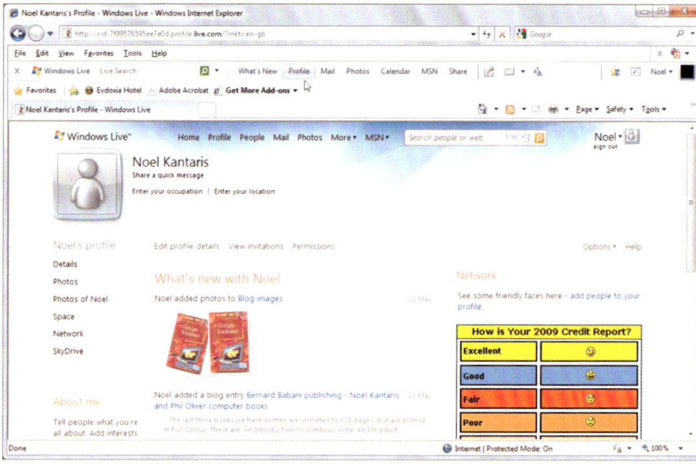

Fig. 8.6 Your Profile Screen

Your Mail Option

Clicking the **Mail** toolbar option, opens your Windows Live Mail, as shown in Fig. 8.7. Again, we show both the first box that opens with your mail messages and the result of clicking the link.

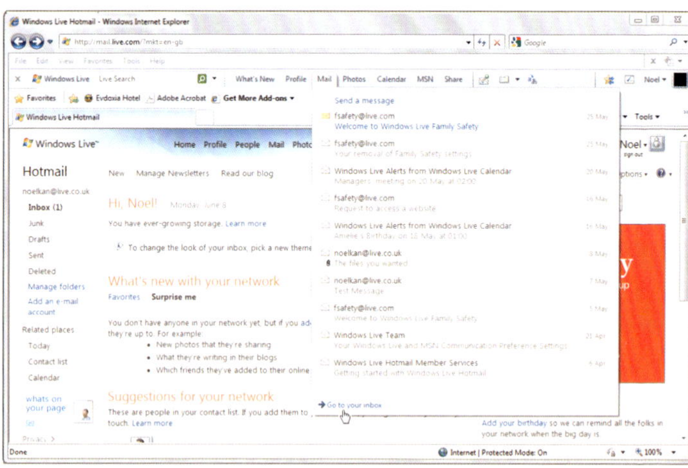

Fig. 8.7 Your Live Mail Screens

From here you can manage newsletters, read blogs, connect to your Hotmail account, see who's on line, and add some people to your network so you can, and they can, see what you are all up to.

The Photos Option

Clicking the **Photos** toolbar button, displays the screen shown in Fig. 8.8 below.

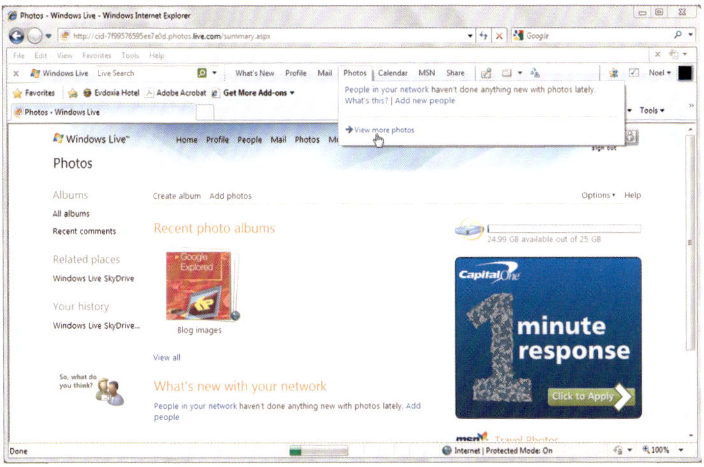

Fig. 8.8 The Photos Option

Here you can see your recent photo albums, and the available space on your **SkyDrive** to which you could upload your photos, videos, blogs, etc., so you could share them with friends and family, so just store them.

The Calendar Option

Clicking the **Calendar** button on the Live Toolbar, might ask you to enter your time zone before loading your Calendar.

Again, when you first click the **Calendar** option on the Live Toolbar, a small calendar is displayed, but clicking the link, causes it to load and display the full version of the application, as shown with both displays open in Fig. 8.9 on the next page.

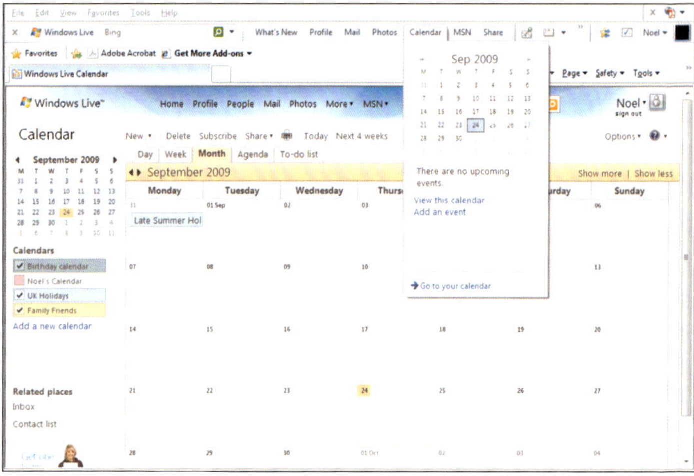

Fig. 8.9 The Calendar Option Screens

We have covered **Calendar** fully in Chapter 5, so we will not pursue it here any further.

The MSN Option

Clicking the MSN option on the Live Toolbar displays the window shown at the top-right of Fig. 8.10, and following the link displays the full screen shown below.

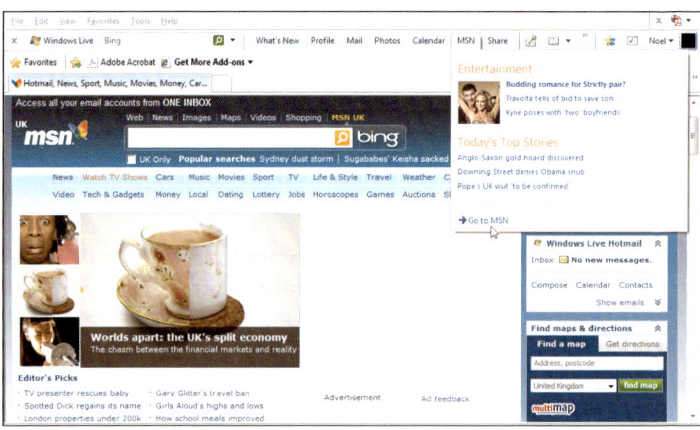

Fig. 8.10 The MSN Option Screens

The Share Option

You can share Web pages with friends and family – the group of people you communicate with and share information with, including those you have added to your Profile and Messenger.

When you add **Favorites** in the **Shared Favorites** folder on Windows Live **SkyDrive**, people in your network can see them in your **What 's new** list which appears in your **Profile** and **Mail**.

Fig. 8.11 below shows the Share screens open on the same screen dump.

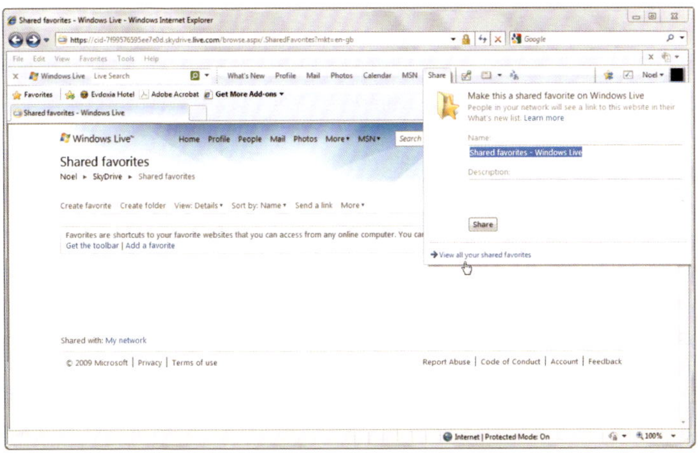

Fig. 8.11 The Share Option Screens

Other Toolbar Options

Additional option buttons on the Live Toolbar give you access to **Live Search Maps** . To **Get news from MSN**, click the button on the Live Toolbar. Clicking the down-arrow on this button displays a list of 30 current news items that you could read at your leisure. These two facilities are discussed next in a bit more detail.

Live Maps

Live Maps allows you to find maps of even small hamlets in the UK and a bit larger ones abroad. When you first click the **Live Search Maps** button on the Live Toolbar, the screen in Fig. 8.12 is displayed.

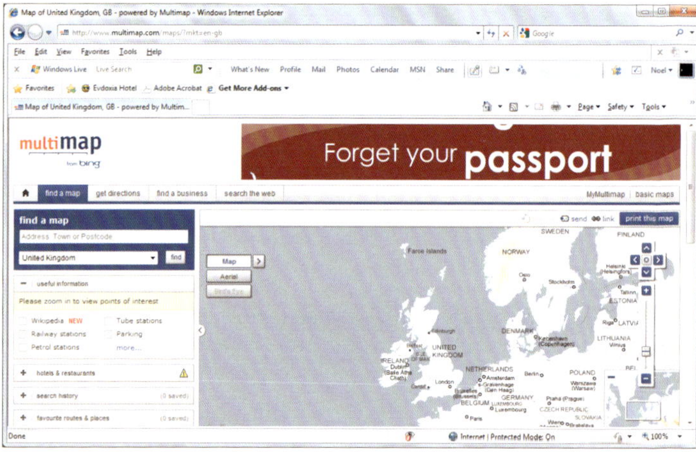

Fig. 8.12 The Search Maps Option Screen

Below we entered the name of a small Hamlet in West Cornwall, called Trevarth, then clicked the **Find** link. Note that you have the choice of displaying two more types of maps; Ordnance Survey (as in Fig. 8.14), and Aerial (as in Fig. 8.15), both shown on the next page. You are even given the name of the nearest railway station.

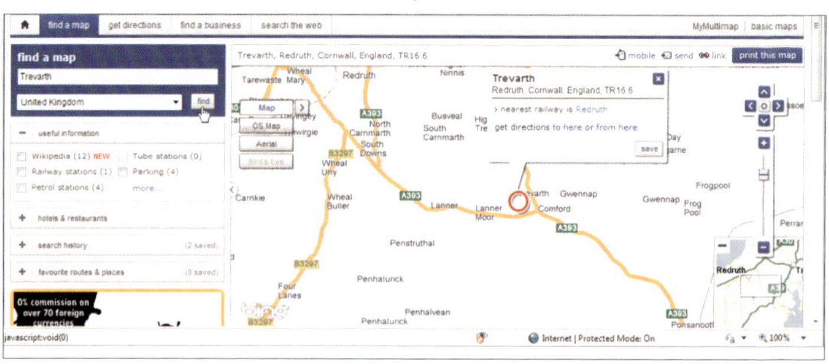

Fig. 8.13 The Road Map of the Searched Area

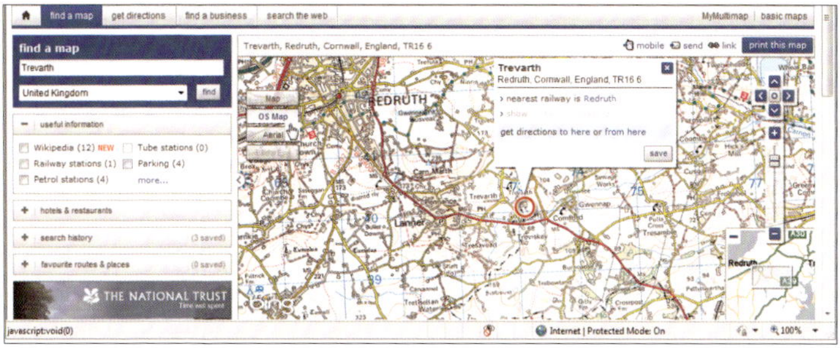

Fig. 8.14 The OS Map of the Searched Area

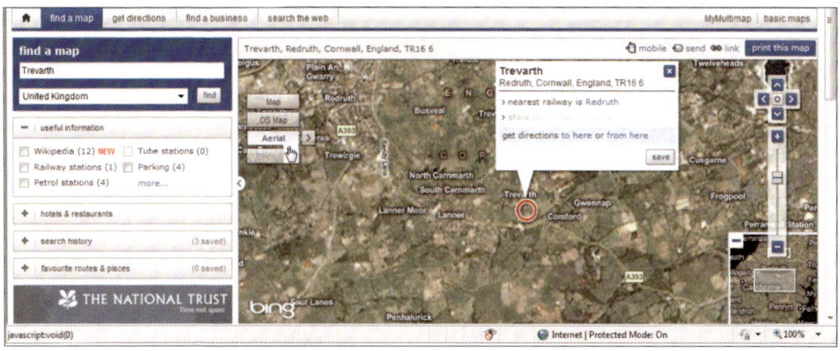

Fig. 8.15 The Aerial Map of the Searched Area

We find these maps quite impressive! Further, on the left of each map display you can find varying useful information, including the location of petrol stations and parking areas.

At the top of each map there is a window in which you can request directions from one location to another, while at the right of each map there are navigation buttons to move your viewing area to an adjoining location.

Getting News from MSN

Clicking the **Get news from MSN** button on the Live Toolbar, and selecting the first item on the list, displays the screen shown in Fig. 8.16 on the next page. On the same screen we show the list of today's news topics that display when you click the down arrow on the button. You can select any of these links to read its contents in more detail, as shown in Fig. 8.17, also shown on the next page.

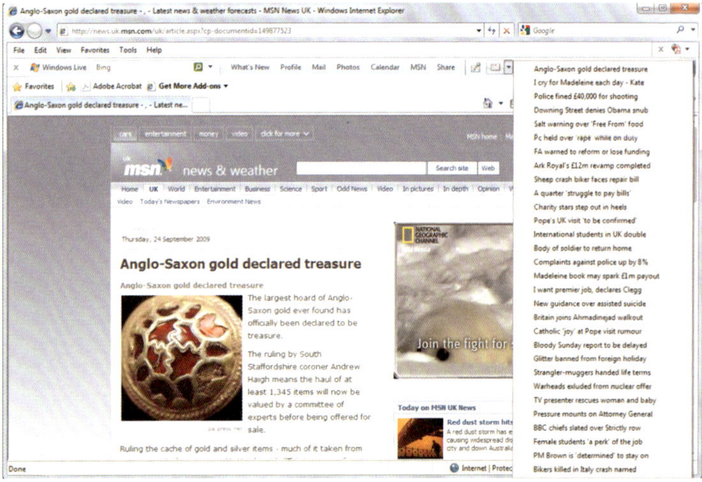

Fig. 8.16 The Get News from MSN Screens

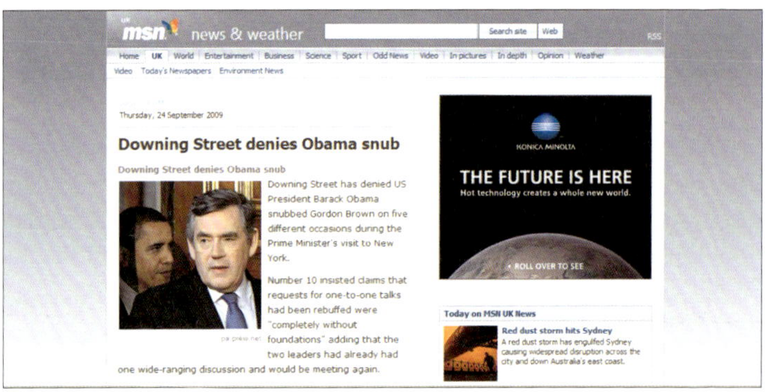

Fig. 8.17 Reading News on MSN

Finally, you can choose to translate a Web page from one language to another, synchronise your favourites across multiple computers, or add buttons to Windows Live Toolbar. We leave it to you to explore these additional facilities, so try them and see where it leads you. Enjoy!

9

Microsoft Security Essentials

Microsoft Security Essentials is a free suite of programs which is made available to all genuine Windows XP, Vista, and Windows 7 users. It comes in both 32-bit and 64-bit versions, except for Windows XP which only come with the 32-bit version.

Microsoft created its Security Essentials application to provide security against viruses and malware for PCs that are not protected with such products, because many first-time users don't activate time-limited programs that are supplied with new PCs, or others, particularly those in emerging countries, can't afford to pay for security programs, most of which need to be renewed yearly.

To download the Microsoft Security Essentials, start Internet Explorer and go to:

www.microsoft.com/downloads/

Next, locate **Microsoft Security Essentials**, and click the **Download** button to start a Wizard which steps you through the installation process. After the Welcome and License agreement screens, the Wizard displays the Windows Validations screen, as shown in Fig. 9.1.

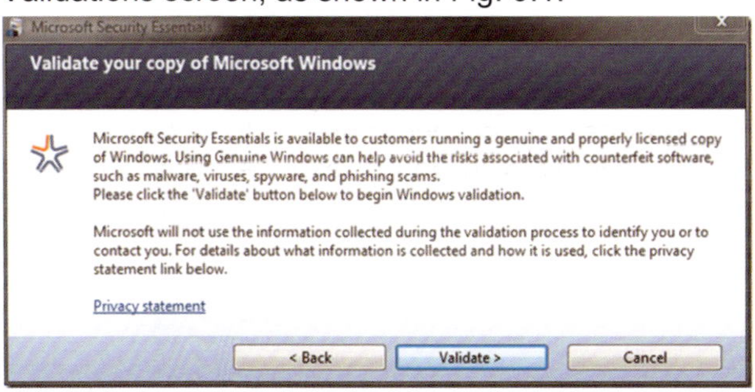

Fig. 9.1

Unless you have genuine Windows software running on your computer, the validation process will fail and Security Essentials will not install. If validation is successful, the screen in Fig. 9.2 is displayed.

Fig. 9.2 Warning Relating to Running Antivirus Programs

Essentially you are warned that running multiple antivirus programs might cause a conflict, and you are advised to disable them before proceeding.

Once installation is complete, you are directed to automatic virus and spyware definition updates, before you are asked to scan your computer, as shown in Fig. 9.3.

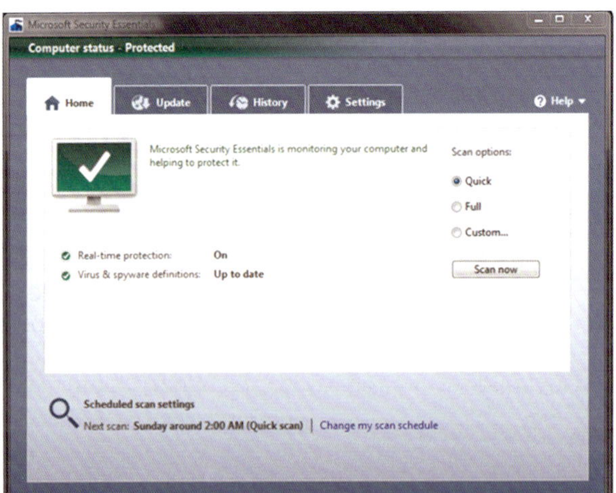

Fig. 9.3

You have three scanning options; Quick, Full or Custom. We suggest that if you haven't scanned your computer before, to select the Full option, even though it takes longer to complete.

Scheduling a Scan Regime

To schedule a scan click the **Change My Scan Schedule** link on the Home window to open the screen of Fig. 9.4.

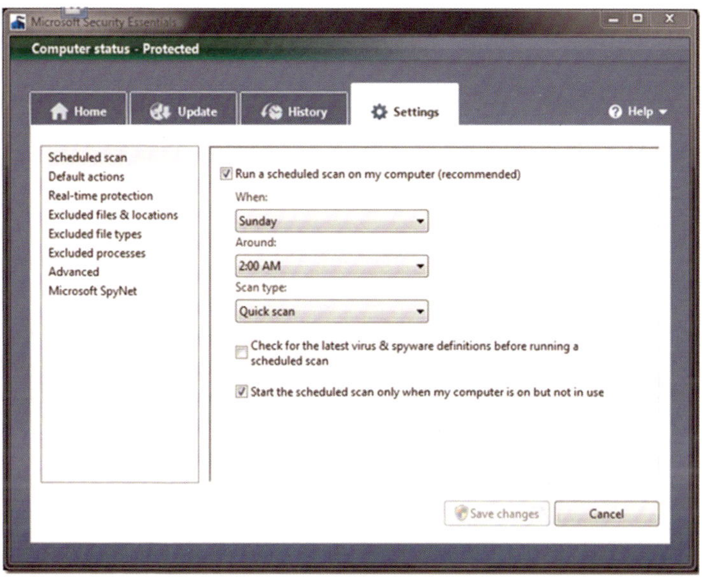

Fig. 9.4 Selecting Scan Options

We suggest you work your way through all the options offered in the left-hand pane and select what is suitable for yourself. Perhaps after the first 'Full' scan of your computer you could select a 'Quick' scan for all subsequent occasions. You could also select a suitable time for when these scans should take place.

The History Tab Screen

To see all **Detected Items**, **Quarantined Items**, and **Allowed Items**, click the History tab, as shown in Fig. 9.5 below.

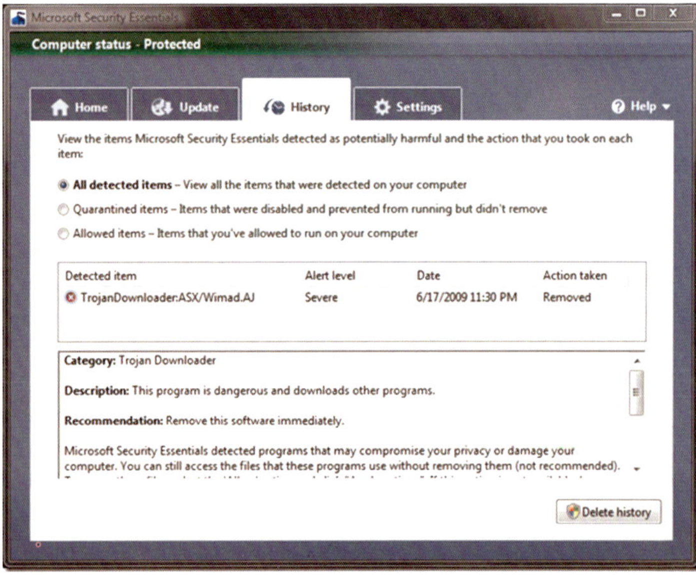

Fig. 9.5 The History Tab Screen

To remove all history, click the **Delete History** button at the bottom of the above screen.

As Microsoft Security Essentials doesn't include a Firewall, do remember to enable the Windows Firewall, by using the **Start**, **Control Panel** option and selecting the **System and Security** entry from the displayed screen. Make sure that under **Security**, the Windows Firewall is active. Also while you are there, enable the Windows Update option, if not already enabled.

10

Office Outlook Connector

If you have Microsoft Office 2003 or 2007 and are using the version of Microsoft Outlook that came with these two versions of Office for receiving e-mail messages, and accessing your contacts and Calendar entries, then Windows Outlook Connector is a must for you.

If you have downloaded Windows Outlook Connector with the other Windows Live Applications, you can skip the next few paragraphs. If not, exit Microsoft Outlook, start Internet Explorer and go to:

http://download.live.com/

Next, locate **Microsoft Office Outlook Connector**, under **Additional Programs**, download it and follow the on-screen instructions.

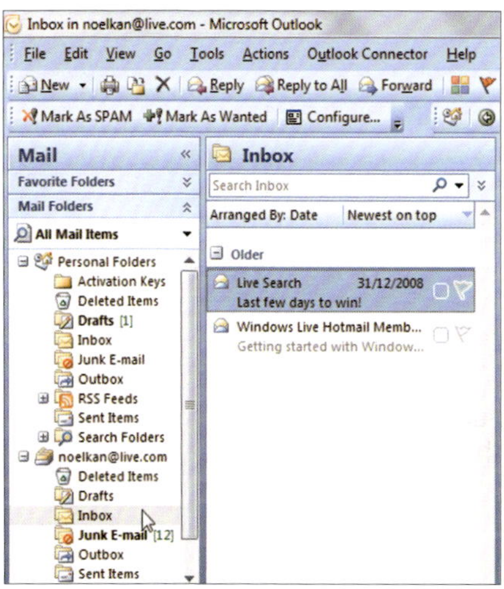

Fig. 10.1 The Live Account Folders and Inbox Contents

Next time you start Microsoft Outlook it will ask you to configure Outlook Connector by entering your e-mail address, your password, and your name as you want it to appear on the recipients Inbox.

After Outlook opens, your Windows Live Mail (or Hotmail) account appears in the Navigation Pane, as pointed to in Fig. 10.1.

Getting Help

To find out what you can do with Office Outlook Connector, click its menu entry, as shown in Fig. 10.2 and select the Help topic **Learn about Windows Live and Outlook**.

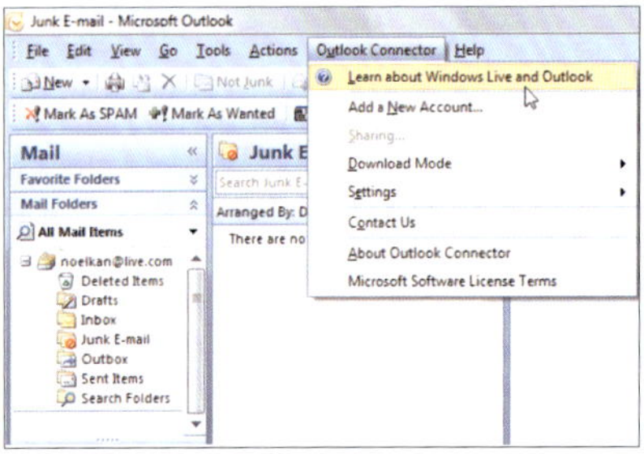

Fig. 10.2 Getting Help with Outlook Connector

This opens the screen shown in Fig. 10.3 below, displaying all the help topics you might want to know.

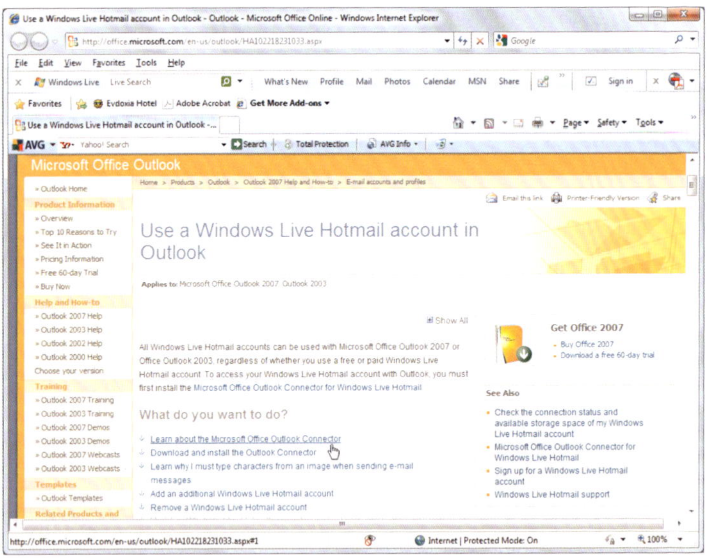

Fig. 10.3 The Microsoft Outlook Help Screen

From here you choose the links to help you find more information. For example, clicking the **Learn about the Microsoft Office Outlook Connector** link pointed to in Fig. 10.3 takes you to the help page associated with that link.

On the left pane of the Help screen on Fig. 10.3, you can also see help links to the various versions of Outlook, but do remember that the only ones relevant to the Outlook Connector are those associated with Outlook 2003 and 2007.

Adding a New Web-based Account

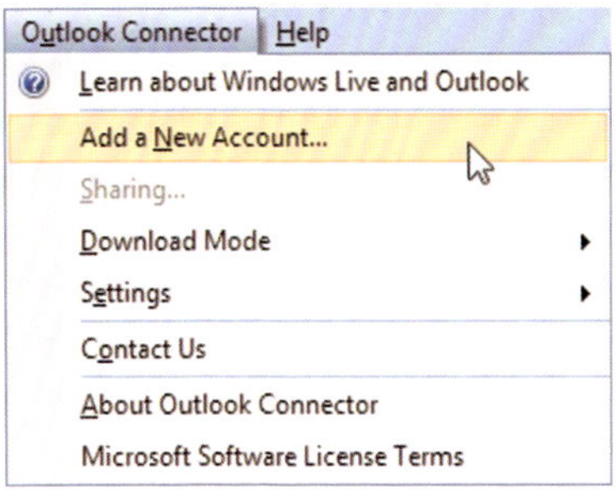

Fig. 10.4 Adding a New Account

To add a new account to Outlook, such as one using Hotmail, click the **Add a New Account** sub-menu of the **Outlook Connector** option. This opens a screen in which you are asked to type in the address of the Web-based account you want Outlook to synchronise with your existing accounts, as shown here in Fig. 10.5.

Fig. 10.5 Adding a New Account

Here we added a Gmail account – it could have been a Hotmail one – with its password and the name that should appear in the recipient's Inbox. Clicking the **OK** button displays a box with the information shown in Fig. 10.6.

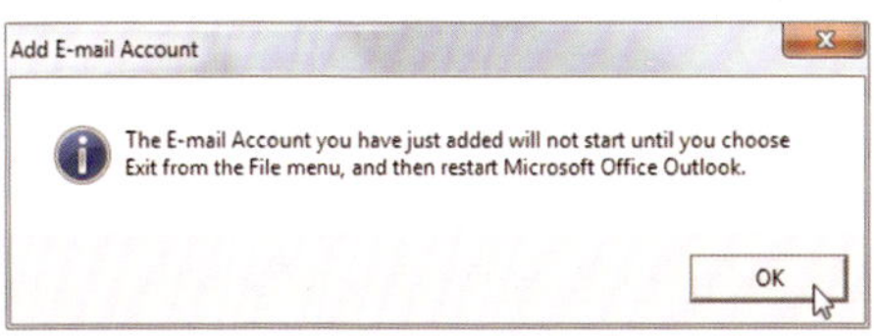

Fig. 10.6 The Add E-mail Account Information Box

Restarting Outlook displays a further dialogue box asking you to **Sign in**. In the displayed box, change the e-mail address from the one offered to you to your **Live** e-mail address, and type the appropriate password, as shown here in Fig. 10.7. The message at the bottom of the screen refers to the attempt made by Outlook to sign you in using the offered e-mail address of the account you were trying to add to Outlook (the Gmail address in our case). Having changed the e-mail address and typed the password, click the **Sign in** button.

Fig. 10.7 Adding a New Account

It is imperative that you wait while Outlook synchronises with the new account and downloads any messages from it. Keep an eye on the right-hand corner of Outlook's Status bar, and when the download finishes you will be ready to open the newly created folder of the new account on the Folders list, as shown here in Fig. 10.8.

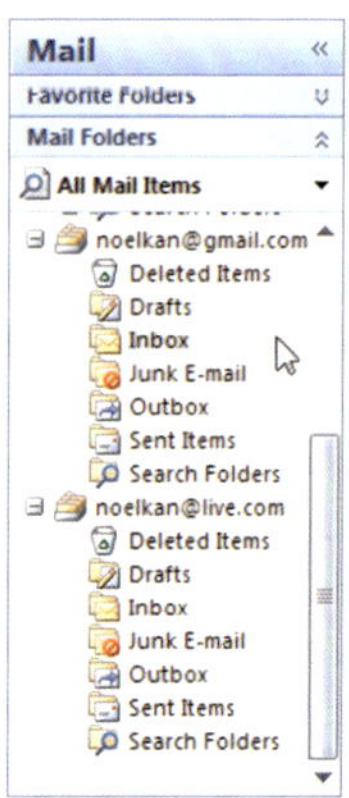

Fig. 10.8 The New Account in the Folders List

Removing an Account from the Folders List

If you were impatient and tried to open the new account folder before synchronisation and downloading was completed, then attempting to open the newly created account folder results in an error. If that is the case, you must remove this account from the Folders list and start again from the beginning.

To remove an account, for any reason, from the Folders list, do the following:

- Click the **Start** button and select **Control Panel**.
- In **Control Panel** click the **User Accounts and Family Safety** link shown here.

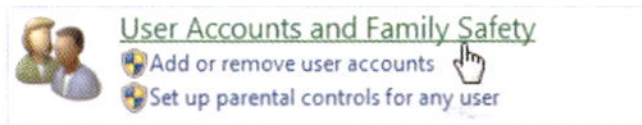

- In the displayed screen, click the **Mail** icon, as shown in Fig. 10.9.

Fig. 10.9 The Control Panel User Accounts and Safety Screen

- In the Mail Setup - Outlook box, shown in Fig. 10.10, click the **E-mail Accounts** button to open the screen shown in Fig. 10.11 on the next page.

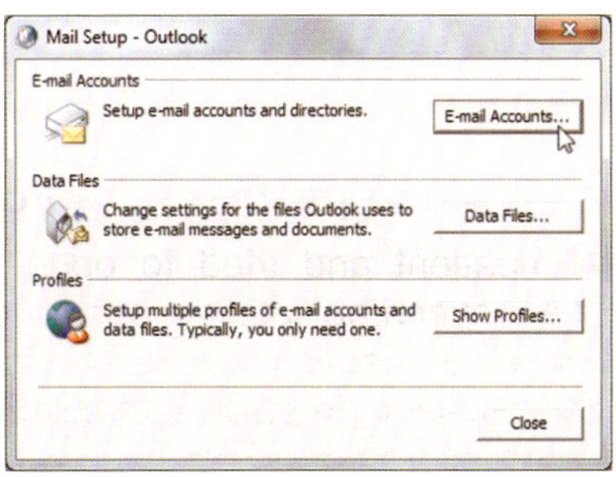

Fig. 10.10 The Mail Setup - Outlook Box

- On the displayed screen, shown below, select the account to be removed and click the **Remove** button.

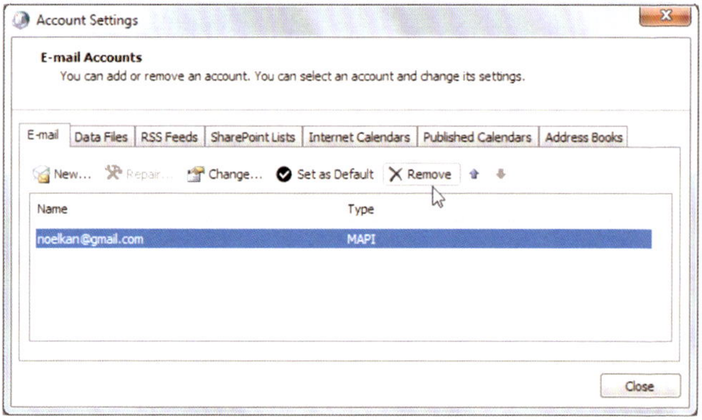

Fig. 10.11 Removing an E-mail Account

E-mail Downloading Modes

Another useful option available in Outlook Connector is the choice of what you want to download, as shown in Fig. 10.12.

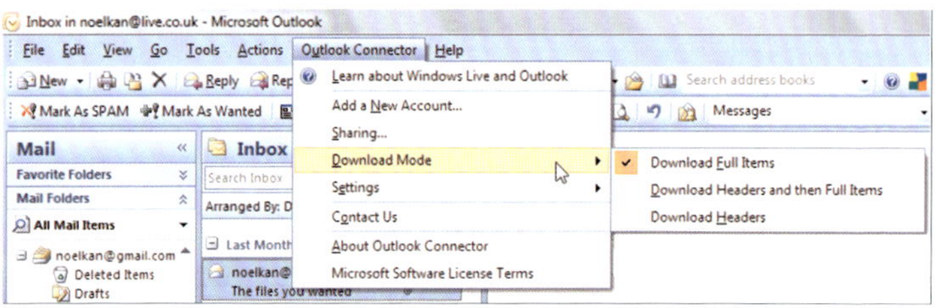

Fig. 10.12 Choosing a Download Mode

As you can see, you can choose between downloading 'Full Items', 'Headers and then Full Items', or just 'Headers'. We leave it to you to investigate the advantages of each of these choices.

That's all the available space allocated for this book. We hope we have given you sufficient basic knowledge to be able to forge ahead by yourselves!

Index